Praise for *Breaking Ground, Breaking Glass Ceilings*

◆◆◆◆◆◆◆◆◆◆◆◆◆◆

"Tammie Ross has created a relevant guide for anyone striving to make a name for themselves in the construction industry. She has weaved her experience into authentic stories that are universally applicable to both men and women, encouraging readers to embrace who they are in a way that leads to success in their personal and professional lives. Tammie Ross takes her unique perspective and puts it into a fun and powerful narrative that is easy to read."

—Jennifer Castenson, Vice President, Buildxact, Contributing Writer, Forbes

"Tammie Ross' book serves as an excellent blueprint for anyone looking to make their mark in corporate America or launch their own business. Her insights are invaluable for crafting a strategic plan that leads to success. She hits the nail on the head in terms of the importance of excellence, networking, and managerial courage. No matter your industry, her guidance is relevant."

—Renee Rhem, VP, Customer Advocacy Department, Subaru of America, Inc.

"Tammie Ross is a rare visionary whose work goes beyond structures, touching the heart of community, culture, and resilience. As a trailblazer her leadership challenges us to imagine a future where our built environments reflect diversity, strength, and beauty of all people. Her contributions are a testament to the limitless potential of those who follow in her footsteps. Tammie Ross' book is a must read! The information within the pages will help you step into your power."

—Gina Neely, TV Personality, Celebrity Chef and Award-Winning Author

"This book is a roadmap for anyone ready to shatter limits and embrace greatness. Tammie Ross goes beyond theory, offering actionable tools, inspiring stories, and invaluable resources that empower readers to be persistent and claim their seat at the table. The strategies presented are comprehensive ensuring success feels as sustainable as it is empowering. Whether you're just starting out or looking to level up, this guide will give you the confidence and practical steps to break through barriers and redefine success. A must-read for trailblazers everywhere!"

—**Dr. Virnitia J. Dixon,** C-Suite Executive of Diversity and Culture and Bestselling Author of *Passion Without Purpose Is...An A-Z Guide of Positive Affirmations*

"This book celebrates the strength, innovation, and resilience of those pushing for change. It's a reminder that success and leadership can transcend gender expectations. The book emphasizes the power of community in overcoming systemic hurdles. It's a powerful reminder that no matter your gender or the industry you're in, fostering inclusivity and supporting each other is essential to driving meaningful change. This book is a must-read for anyone interested in understanding the dynamics of gender in the workplace, regardless of the field you're in."

—**Justin Q. Williams,** Designer, Trademark Design Co.

"This invaluable resource is a profound and practical exploration of resilience, emotional intelligence, and equity in male-dominated industries. By blending personal narratives with actionable strategies, Ross equips readers with tools to address sexism, microaggressions, and the challenges of intersectionality while fostering inclusive environments. Her reflections on emotional intelligence and the transformative power of mentorship, sponsorship, and supportive networks offer invaluable guidance for navigating complex workplace dynamics."

—**Sandra Rosa,** Chief Human Resources Officer

"Mrs. Ross' book is truly inspirational for professionals in a variety of careers. In particular, the history of her three-decade career trajectory is filled with lessons of perseverance and persistence. In her book, she describes how success is often achieved when one steps out of one's comfort zone to be daring, and she provides a roadmap for people to do the same with their careers."

—**Andrew Assadollahi, Ph.D., P.E.,** Dean of the Gadomski School of Engineering, Christian Brothers University

"Tammie Ross hits this out of the park. It is refreshing to see someone so committed to reaching new heights. The Ross' exemplify Patience, Perseverance, Passion and Polish! I have enjoyed watching Tammie Ross grow and am excited for what she does in the future."

—**Dave Moore,** President, CGP, CAPS1, CAPS2, 2024 President Home Builders Association of Tennessee, 2018 President West TN Home Builders Association, The Dave Moore Companies

"It's all here. An inspiring story of resilience and the lessons learned along the way to help other women navigate their way to a successful career on their own terms. Tammie Ross shares many gems that encourages self-reflection and action planning for personal growth."

—**Financial Executive**

Breaking Ground, Breaking Glass Ceilings

A Guide to Finding Success in Male-Dominated Industries

TAMMIE ROSS

Breaking Ground, Breaking Glass Ceilings:
A Guide for Finding Success in Male-Dominated Industries
BuilderBooks, a Service of the National Association of Home Builders (NAHB)

Patricia Potts	Senior Director, Publisher
CSBWrites	Editor
Circle Graphics, Inc.	Cover Design
Circle Graphics, Inc.	Composition

James W. Tobin III	NAHB Chief Executive Officer
John McGeary	NAHB SVP, Business Development & Growth Strategy

Disclaimer

This publication provides accurate information on the subject matter covered. The publisher is selling it with the understanding that the publisher is not providing legal, accounting, or other professional service. If you need legal advice or other expert assistance, obtain the services of a qualified professional experienced in the subject matter involved. The NAHB has used commercially reasonable efforts to ensure that the contents of this volume are complete and appear without error; however, the NAHB makes no representations or warranties regarding the accuracy and completeness of this document's contents. The NAHB specifically disclaims any implied warranties of merchantability or fitness for a particular purpose. The NAHB shall not be liable for any loss of profit or any other commercial damages, including but not limited to incidental, special, consequential, or other damages. Reference herein to any specific commercial products, process, or service by trade name, trademark, manufacturer, or otherwise does not necessarily constitute or imply its endorsement, recommendation, or favored status by the NAHB. The views and opinions of the author expressed in this publication do not necessarily state or reflect those of the NAHB, and they shall not be used to advertise or endorse a product.

Published in the United States of America

29 28 27 26 25   1 2 3 4 5

ISBN: 978-0-86718-819-6
eISBN: 978-0-86718-820-2

For further information, please contact:
National Association of Home Builders
1201 15th Street, NW
Washington, DC 20005-2800
BuilderBooks.com

Dedication

This book is dedicated to my husband, unwavering mentor, and dearest friend, Roderick Ross. Rod, your steadfast support, selfless sacrifices, and unyielding belief in my potential have been the pillars of our journey. Your hard work provided the foundation for me to pursue education and dare to dream beyond conventional boundaries. This book is a testament to our shared triumphs, the challenges we conquered together, and the love that fueled it all.

Table of Contents

Preface

Throughout history, the metaphor of the "glass ceiling" has symbolized the invisible yet formidable barriers that prevent certain groups—especially women and minorities—from reaching the upper echelons of corporate leadership, regardless of their qualifications or achievements. This phenomenon, pervasive across industries, is being increasingly challenged as society progresses, with trailblazers paving the way for future generations. By breaking these barriers, we do more than shatter a ceiling; we unlock a universe of opportunities, inspiring generations to aspire to greater heights.

The history of women in construction is rich and varied, stretching back to the Middle Ages. Records from 13th-century Spain indicate women laborers working on construction sites, and throughout the centuries, women have continued to contribute to this field, often without recognition. The Industrial Revolution saw women entering the paid workforce in greater numbers, and during World War II, women filled many construction, mechanical, and technical jobs while many men served overseas.[1] Despite these contributions, women remain significantly underrepresented in the construction workforce, particularly in the trades.

Today, the storyline is evolving from merely breaking barriers to constructing ladders of opportunity for all. According to the U.S. Equal Employment Opportunity Commission, women face considerable challenges in the construction industry. This scarcity of women has profound implications for the economy and the sustainability of the industry, which struggles with recruitment challenges and an aging workforce amid rising construction demands.

Although the construction industry has traditionally been male-dominated, recent trends show a gradual increase in female representation. As of December 2023, women comprised 10.8% of the workforce within the U.S. construction industry, with a smaller percentage of 4.3% working specifically in construction trades. Despite these gains, women of color remain significantly underrepresented. Efforts to address the underlying factors contributing to this disparity, such as unconscious gender bias, lack of training opportunities, and persistent stereotypes, are crucial for fostering an inclusive environment that enables all individuals to thrive in the construction sector.[2]

In addition to construction, women's representation in other male-dominated industries such as engineering, information technology, and aerospace also reflects a significant gender gap. In engineering, women make up only about 15% of the workforce.[3] The information technology sector sees women holding around 24% of computing jobs. In the aerospace industry, women's participation has fluctuated around 20% for at least 30 years, with only 11% of astronauts being women.[4] The automotive industry also shows a disparity, with women accounting for approximately 27% of the US auto manufacturing workforce.[5]

These statistics not only highlight the underrepresentation of women but also the need for a concerted effort to create inclusive environments that encourage and support women's participation and advancement in these fields. By addressing these disparities, we can unlock the full potential of half the world's population, fostering innovation, and driving economic growth.

This book is written to be a guiding light for women navigating the challenges of male-dominated industries. It offers strategies, insights, and inspiration to empower women to break ground and shatter ceilings, paving the way for a more equitable and prosperous future.

Introduction

In the enduring words of Andrew Carnegie, "Anything worth having is worth working for"—and the path to becoming a general contractor has indeed been full of hard work. Within these pages, you will embark on a journey transcending mere architectural plans and solid foundations. It is a journey that reaches the heart of resilience and ambition, where every hammer and nail is not just about building structures but about forging a legacy in a world that often resists change.

The construction industry—where blueprints come alive, where walls rise, and where ceilings hold both dreams and limitations—has been my testing ground. It is an industry fraught with challenges yet brimming with promise. Our first home, acquired through diligent saving, was our first trial. We learned valuable lessons about homeownership and resilience, navigating pitfalls, and advocating for ourselves.

During my 20+ year career in the automotive finance industry, I navigated boardrooms and leadership circles predominantly occupied by men, often finding myself as the only person of color in these spaces. This journey has not only shaped my professional outlook but also instilled in me a profound sense of responsibility to mentor and uplift others. I have mentored several individuals, sharing my knowledge to help them navigate their careers. Leading high-performing teams, I focused on developing talent and assisting others in their career progression, fostering an environment where diversity is acknowledged and celebrated.

In these pages, you will discover more than strategies for success. You will explore the transformative power of emotional intelligence—the ability to navigate human connections. And you will witness the art of community-centric leadership, where every voice matters.

Whether you are a seasoned professional in a male-dominated industry, an aspiring home builder, or a dreamer with a blueprint in hand, this book invites you to break ground—to shatter ceilings, construct networks, and build a future where every woman's voice echoes through the scaffolding of progress.

"Breaking Ground, Breaking Glass Ceilings" is a narrative of breaking barriers and constructing legacies. Its purpose is to empower and inspire you. As you turn the pages of this book, you are invited to join me on this extraordinary journey of building not just structures but a future where every woman's ambition is the blueprint for success.

From glass ceilings to growth mindsets, mentorship to mindfulness, these chapters, plus the takeaways and reflections, hold the keys to empowerment.

Welcome to "Breaking Ground." Let's lay the foundation for something extraordinary.

◆◆◆◆◆◆◆◆◆◆◆◆◆◆◆◆◆

PART I

Beyond Limits, Pursuing Dreams

When we break through glass ceilings, we are not just elevating ourselves; we are lifting all who dare to dream. – Tammie Ross

CHAPTER 1

Chasing Dreams
Against All Odds

◆◆◆◆◆◆◆◆◆◆◆◆◆◆

I grew up in Memphis, Tennessee, in a traditional one-level house less than ten minutes from Graceland, Elvis Presley's home. Our house had three bedrooms, one and a half bathrooms, a small galley kitchen, and a living room that featured my dad's favorite reclining leather chair. It was clean and comfortable but lacked decorative touches. To bring some décor into my personal space, I painted the walls of my bedroom and added wallpaper borders.

At 12 years old, I found solace and inspiration in artistry, which became a refuge from life's chaos. I took great joy in transforming the bare walls of my bedroom with beautiful images, each telling a story born from my imagination. The scent of fresh paint became a symbol of creation, a sensory reminder of the power I held within my fingertips.

I took art classes throughout middle and high school and painted beautiful pictures that my mother proudly displayed on the walls of our home. Yet, it was not on an artist's fabric canvas that I found my true canvas. It was within the walls of houses that dreams took shape. The quiet moments between brushstrokes and color palettes revealed a passion— the art of creating spaces. These spaces held stories, aspirations, and the resolve to overcome challenges.

The Kirkland's Home store was a cherished haven of creativity for me. It captured my fascination. Accompanied by my mother, I regularly explored its treasure-filled aisles, each visit deepening my passion for decor and design. The textures, patterns, and hues spoke to me, revealing secrets of transitional décor and emerging trends. This early exposure to the art of decorating shaped my future career path.

I eagerly awaited my sixteenth birthday, which marked my eligibility to work at Kirkland's. My time there was transformative. It offered me hands-on experience in interior decor and allowed me to express my creativity through design projects. I learned how to wrap presents, create tablescapes for display, and design mock living rooms with rugs, throw pillows and chairs. I thrived in curating spaces that reflected my unique style, with each season bringing new opportunities to transform our home's spaces with vitality and character.

With the money I earned at Kirkland's and the benefit of my generous discount, I purchased decorative pieces for my childhood home. I carefully selected throw pillows in vibrant colors and intricate patterns, each adding a touch of personality to our living room.

I also bought a beautifully crafted, silver-backed hand mirror for my mother. Its unique design was both timeless and elegant, with delicate engravings that brought a sense of sophistication. I knew it would perfectly complement the antique makeup vanity she had inherited from her grandmother. It warms my heart that, 30 years later, my mom still cherishes that mirror.

I met my husband, Rod, in the summer of 1993 while working as a waitress at Red Lobster during college. After we married, we experienced the ups and downs of renting various properties in inner-city Memphis. Each rental came with its share of issues, and we dreamed of owning our own home, a safe haven for our growing family.

After diligently saving for two and a half years, Rod and I were finally able to buy our first home in 1997. It was a charming, two-story house on Egan Drive, straight out of a storybook. The house had a white picket fence and a magnificent oak tree that cast its shade across the property. The windows were beautifully placed throughout, and a quiet office space connected to the kitchen quickly became my sanctuary for journaling, paying bills, and reading after the house had quieted down. We purchased this lovely home for $99,000.

This accomplishment was particularly significant given my husband's background. He grew up in public housing and didn't even realize as a child that his family lived in the Kansas Court Projects. All he knew was that he was part of a tight-knit community of families who always looked out for each other. They didn't have much, but they had one another. Holidays were a special time for Rod, knowing his mother would cook something extra delicious with the seasonal foods. Thanksgiving was his favorite, as the entire family would come together to enjoy the meals his mother spent all night preparing. Despite the cramped quarters, the house buzzed with warmth and family, and Rod dreamed of one day owning his own home—one big enough to welcome all the people he loved. From a young age, he had one goal: to buy his mom a house.

Growing up in the projects meant enduring economic hardship. To help, Rod began delivering newspapers at the age of 9, and by 11, he took it upon himself to buy his own clothes and school supplies. His strong work ethic and determination stayed with him, and he eventually became the first person in his family to own a home. Achieving this milestone was a proud realization of the American Dream, and it was a testament to our shared values of hard work and perseverance.

However, our excitement was short-lived. Just two months after we moved in, while I was bathing our two young sons, a tile came loose from the bathtub surround, exposing rotting wood and revealing a termite infestation behind the wall. As Darby, our four-year-old, and Devon, our two-year-old, splashed in the tub, their laughter echoed in the bathroom. Suddenly, a tile popped off, revealing the hidden damage.

Darby's eyes widened in surprise. "Mommy, what's that?" he asked, his voice filled with a mixture of curiosity and concern. He could tell something was wrong.

I tried to stay calm, reassuring him. "It's okay, sweetie. We'll get it fixed." I quickly scooped Devon out of the tub, his little hands still reaching for bubbles, and wrapped him in a towel. His giggles continued, blissfully unaware. Darby, however, was more cautious. His eyes stayed glued to the exposed wall, his young mind working to understand what he was seeing. "Don't worry, Darby," I said with a smile. "Everything's going to be alright."

We had unknowingly purchased a house with many problems. To finance the necessary repairs, we took on part-time jobs in addition to our demanding full-time work. Rod was a salesman at a GMC dealership, where he often worked 10-hour days to support us. Meanwhile, I worked in customer service at First Tennessee Bank in the mortgage department.

Our part-time job was a paper route delivering the "Commercial Appeal" newspaper. Every morning, we woke up at 2:30 a.m., picked up the papers by 3:30 a.m., and delivered them all by 6 a.m. Unfortunately, we had to take our sleeping boys with us on the route. After finishing the deliveries, we'd return home by 6:30 a.m., shower, change, get the boys ready for daycare, and head to work by 8:30 a.m. This routine became unsustainable after six months, as it was taking a physical and mental toll on us, so we stopped the paper route.

Instead, Rod and I reviewed our budget and cut out all non-essential expenses, including dining out and cable television. Rod committed to working two extra hours each day and gave up one of his days off to sell more cars. During this time, we lived without any luxuries. Rod had a $50 weekly allowance, and I had a $25 allowance. Every spare penny went toward the repairs on our home. We felt betrayed by the hidden decay that had undermined our sense of safety and sanctuary. I constantly worried about new problems arising and draining us financially.

It took 18 months to complete the repairs. By 1999, with the help of our neighbors, Buster and Cherry, we learned to handle some of the repairs ourselves. Buster, a natural handyman, generously shared his time and knowledge. Sunday afternoons were spent working on projects and hiring contractors for tasks we couldn't manage on our own. We stayed in the house throughout the repairs and eventually sold it at a break-even price, vowing never to buy an existing home again.

In 2000, we purchased a new home from a mass builder and paid a premium for a desirable lot. We were thrilled to move in and even had the chance to personalize a few features from the builder's showroom, such as plumbing fixtures, cabinet knobs, paint, carpet, and tile. This bit of customization was exciting.

However, we soon discovered that another house would be built directly in front of ours in the next phase of development—we had unknowingly bought a flag lot. Our disputes with the builder went nowhere, and we realized, too late, that we could have avoided this by requesting an updated plat map. Once again, our lack of knowledge had led to housing difficulties.

Despite this, we continued to learn from our experiences. During this time, we met BJ, a contractor, whom we hired, through sweat equity, to help us finish an expandable area in our home, turning it into a beautiful bedroom for Darby and Devon. We gave it a transportation theme, with a red car bed for Darby and a blue one for Devon. We even created a reading nook with bean bags, which the boys adored.

Fortunately, two years later, we sold the house and looked for a more suitable location. Our third home, purchased in 2003, was also a new build by a mass builder. This time, armed with greater knowledge, we selected one of the best lots in the neighborhood and collaborated with the builder to improve the floor plan. The house was located at the entrance of a quiet cove, with a field of mature trees behind us that could not be developed, providing a beautiful backdrop. For the first time, we could leave the blinds open and wake up to the sun shining through, greeting us with the promise of a new day.

This new home reflected our evolving tastes and growing expertise. We added a second fireplace, expanded the closets into a shared space, converted the second closet into an office, and expanded the dining room for an open-concept feel—before it became trendy. We also added niches to display art in a hallway that would otherwise have been a bare wall. We would gather ideas from design magazines and share them with the builder. Our design choices were so successful that the builder replicated them in 59 other houses. This home marked our growth as homeowners, turning our past mistakes into valuable lessons.

Motivated by a desire to avoid past errors and a newfound love for property and construction, Rod and I entered the real estate industry in 2003. Between 2003 and 2007, we dove into the world of new home construction, acquiring a wealth of knowledge. I partnered with experienced real estate agents who guided me, and I joined the Memphis Area Association of Realtors to network and stay informed on market trends. Rod and I also visited construction sites, immersing ourselves in learning the ins and outs of building a home.

By 2007, we took a significant step and personally oversaw the building of our first custom home. I'll never forget the day we found the lot that would become our home. We were attending a dinner party with friends in a beautiful neighborhood in Cordova, Tennessee, a place we didn't think we could afford. As we turned a corner in the neighborhood, we saw a young man placing a "For Sale by Owner" sign in the yard. We knew it was meant to be. The young man was eager to sell quickly and priced the lot below market value. We canceled our dinner plans and put the lot under contract.

We held onto the lot for a few months while gathering subcontractors and designing our custom home. We clipped pictures of features we wanted and worked with an architect to bring our vision to life. The result was a beautifully designed home, one of Rod's favorites to this day. My favorite feature was the coved ceiling in the foyer, inspired by ancient Roman architecture, which we both admired. Our first custom home became a masterpiece, and I am incredibly proud of what we created.

Building our home was an inspiring and transformative experience. As an artist, designing and building the home allowed me to express our vision in a tangible way, which was deeply fulfilling. For Rod, it represented a significant accomplishment—creating a home that would hold no hidden surprises. The process taught us resilience, patience, and confidence in our abilities, sparking a passion for helping others achieve their construction dreams.

Foundations of Resilience:
Navigating Homeownership's Trials

The journey through our housing challenges was not just a series of transactions or construction projects; it was an emotional odyssey that tested our resilience, our marriage, and our very dreams. The first home we bought was supposed to be a sanctuary, a place where laughter and love would echo through the halls. Instead, it became a source of stress and sleepless nights. The dislodged tile in the bathroom was like a crack in our hopes, and the termites behind it were eating away at our hard-earned stability.

The part-time job we took on to finance the repairs were more than just additional work; they were a weight on our shoulders, a constant reminder of the vulnerability of our aspirations. We felt the sting of injustice, the frustration of being misled, and the exhaustion that comes from juggling multiple responsibilities. Yet, in those moments of despair, we found strength in each other and a determination to overcome the obstacles before us.

Selling our first house was bittersweet. It was a release from the burden of its problems but also a relinquishing of the dreams we had attached to it. The second house, with its obstructed view and the builder's indifference, was another blow to our confidence. It felt as though our voices were unheard, our needs unacknowledged. The realization of our naivety overshadowed the excitement of a new beginning.

However, with each challenge, we learned a lesson. We learned to ask the right questions, to demand transparency, and to never settle for less than what we deserved. Our third home was a confirmation of this growth. It was not just a structure of bricks and mortar; it was a symbol of our learned wisdom, a reflection of our journey from novices to savvy homebuyers.

The emotional toll of these experiences was immense but transformative. The constant stress and financial strain tested both our marriage and patience. There were sleepless nights filled with worry and days when the weight of our responsibilities felt overwhelming. Yet, these challenges ultimately brought us closer. We learned to lean on each other for support, communicate more effectively, and draw strength from our shared goals. This experience taught us resilience and patience, empowering us to believe in our abilities and inspiring us to help others achieve their homeownership dreams.

It shaped us into more than just homeowners; it made us advocates, educators, and, eventually, creators in the world of real estate and construction. The pain of the past became the foundation for a future where we could help others avoid the pitfalls we had encountered. It was a crucible that forged our character and our commitment to building not just houses, but homes filled with integrity and love.

CHAPTER 2

Rising Above Barriers and Cultivating Resilience

◆◆◆◆◆◆◆◆◆◆◆◆◆◆

The historical lack of diversity in construction fueled my determination to enter the industry and excel. Each educational milestone was a chance to defy stereotypes and redefine success. My ambition extended beyond innovative designs—I aimed to create legacies that would last beyond the physical structures.

In 2008, Rod and I began working toward our goal of becoming builders. We were riding high on the success of completing our first custom home, but reality set in: we had sons who were 13 and 11, and financial stability was essential. Rod had risen to a well-known and highly respected Finance Director in the automotive industry, and I had entered the industry on the lender side. Together, we ranked in the top 10% of earners in Tennessee, making us the highest earners in both our families. Rod stayed true to his promise of financially supporting his mother, with help from his brother Nikita and sister Joanna. While we were financially stable and happy, we weren't quite brave enough to leave our jobs to pursue our dreams. So, we continued working while I focused on completing my education, always keeping our dream of becoming builders in the back of our minds.

Though a high school diploma and on-the-job training are typically enough to become a general contractor, I decided to go beyond the basics to prepare for the possibility of pursuing our dream. As a woman of color entering the construction industry, I felt compelled to exceed expectations, armed with an education that would make my expertise undeniable. In 2007, I graduated cum laude from Christian Brothers University (CBU), a journey that took longer than expected due to getting married and starting a family as a freshman in college. My spiritual and familial responsibilities made it difficult to finish quickly, but I am grateful for the challenge. After originally attending a public university, Rod encouraged me to push myself and enroll at CBU, a private university. To this day, I use the lessons learned at CBU, and I'm proud I didn't take the easier route. Although it took time to finish, graduating was a memorable moment for me and my family.

During the COVID-19 pandemic in 2020, I used the uncertainty of that time to pursue my MBA in project management from Louisiana State University, which complemented my bachelor's degree in business administration from CBU. The coursework, focused on construction projects, reignited our dream. With our sons grown and us now empty nesters, we finally had the time and space to seriously pursue our aspirations. On December 17, 2021, I graduated with my MBA, cheered on by our adult children, making all the hard work worth it. My academic pursuits equipped me with crucial skills in business management, project management, and strategic planning—essential tools for running a successful business.

In 2022, I earned a Six Sigma Green Belt Certification, which has been instrumental in improving project efficiency, reducing defects, and saving costs while increasing client satisfaction. Earning this certification required mastering the Six Sigma methodology, particularly the DMAIC (Define, Measure, Analyze, Improve, Control) process. This data-driven approach has been invaluable in streamlining processes and reducing risks. I knew this methodology would improve efficiency and help me tackle complex challenges, ultimately enhancing project outcomes. I believe this approach gives Residence by Ross a competitive edge, showcasing our commitment to excellence and continuous improvement.

Driven by my thirst for knowledge, I took on the challenge of the general contractor exam. Despite it being open-book, mastering the content from 18 different books was daunting. Rod and I spent countless evenings and weekends studying, using index cards and leveraging our residential construction experience to grasp building codes and regulations.

My first attempt at the exam was humbling. As the only woman among men, I experienced imposter syndrome. Despite Rod's support and extensive preparation, I failed. However, inspired by Thomas Edison's words, "Many of life's failures are people who did not realize how close they were to success when they gave up," I persisted.

On my fourth attempt, I approached the exam with renewed confidence, embracing my unique perspective as an asset. I requested a separate seating area to minimize distractions and create a focused environment. Six hours and forty-eight minutes later, I passed the general contractor exam!

For me, this victory symbolized breaking barriers and redefining what's possible in the construction industry. In November 2022, Rod and I launched our construction company, Residence by Ross, with me as CEO and Rod as CFO. Our journey is a testament to the power of perseverance. From 2007 to 2023, we honed our skills through personal real estate investments, building and selling homes, and helping family and friends improve their properties.

Our next hurdle was obtaining licensure from the state of Tennessee. This involved passing the required exams, preparing a CPA-verified financial statement, submitting reference letters, proving insurance coverage, and ensuring our LLC met state regulations.

After submitting our application to the Board of Licensing Contractors, we were initially disappointed. Our anticipated contractor's limit of $800,000 was unexpectedly reduced to $25,000. This setback was disheartening, but we refused to let it define us. I revisited the licensing authorities, advocating for a thorough reassessment of my qualifications. The limit was increased to $150,000—an improvement, but still short of our goal to build homes from scratch. Confident in our abilities, I declined this offer.

For our third attempt, we opted for a personal interview with the board. This was our opportunity to articulate the breadth of our experience and the strength of Residence by Ross. During the interview, we shared our story, highlighting the diverse skills and knowledge we had accumulated. The board was receptive to our vision of constructing buildings and crafting exceptional living spaces. Ultimately, we were granted a monetary limit of $780,000, with a 10% tolerance, allowing us to take on projects up to $838,000. This approval was a significant affirmation of our capabilities and a tribute to our commitment to excellence.

The interview was not just a procedural step; it was a turning point. It marked the culmination of years of dedication and strategic growth of Residence by Ross. It was an opportunity to share our passion and to connect with those who held the keys to our future. It opened the door to larger projects and solidified our role in shaping the architectural landscape. Being officially recognized as a general contractor was a dream realized and a prelude to a bright future for our company.

The licensure process was evidence of the complexities of navigating professional landscapes. The initial disappointment was a stark reminder that the road to success is often lined with obstacles. Yet, it was the unwavering belief in our vision and the relentless pursuit of our goals that carried us through.

This journey, with its highs and lows, underscored the importance of resilience, the value of education, and the impact of self-advocacy. It is a story of personal and professional growth, a chronicle of breaking barriers, and proof of the fact that with determination and strategic action, the future is ours to shape.

CHAPTER 3

Shattering Glass Ceilings

◆◆◆◆◆◆◆◆◆◆◆◆◆

After passing the general contractor exam, I became acutely aware of the challenges that lay ahead in an often exclusive, change-resistant industry. For example, I encountered skepticism from potential clients and colleagues who doubted my capabilities. Yet, these challenges only stoked the fires of my determination, serving as the impetus for growth, resilience, and empowerment. As a woman navigating a male-dominated industry, I recognized an undeniable truth: representation matters.

My educational and corporate experiences, including roles as a Regional Sales Director, Vice President of Risk and Compliance, and Director of Strategic Partnerships in the automotive industry, often made me the only woman and person of color in the room. These roles underscored the importance of visibility—of showing up and standing out, not just for oneself, but for all those who would follow. This realization sparked a fervent desire within me to illuminate a path laden with ambitious goals for girls and women who have the audacity to shatter the proverbial glass ceilings.

Now, driven by a mission to infuse diversity and inclusivity into the very fabric of the construction industry, I stand at the forefront of a growing movement. With nearly two decades of experience under my belt, I have navigated numerous challenges and triumphs. For instance, I have led complex residential projects from conception to completion, managed multimillion-dollar budgets, and built a network of trusted subcontractors and suppliers. My aim is nothing short of revolutionary. I envision a residential construction landscape transformed—a realm where opportunities abound, where the capabilities of women are not just recognized but celebrated and sought after.

By sharing my story, I aim to inspire and empower a new generation of builders, architects, electricians, plumbers, and leaders. I strive to foster a world in which aspirations know no gender, where dreams are given wings to soar, and where the sky is not a limit but instead a canvas for our highest ambitions.

We are not just constructing buildings; we are building a legacy. A legacy of equality, of shattered barriers, and of boundless potential. This is more than a personal mission; it is a clarion call to action for an industry, society, and every woman who has ever been told "no." Together, we are not just reshaping skylines; we are redefining what it means to be builders in the truest sense—architects of a future where diversity is not just accepted but expected and where excellence is defined not by gender but by the merit of our work and the integrity of our character.

My goal in sharing my story is to demonstrate what is possible when women dare to dream big and work tirelessly toward fulfilling those dreams. It is a story of overcoming, transcending limits, and paving the way for others to rise, shine, lead, and transform the world—one beam, brick, and glass ceiling at a time.

The Power of Belief and Authenticity

I am a "girlie girl" at heart. I adore blingy, high-heeled shoes, shimmering accessories, and fashion-forward attire and let's not forget how a Louis Vuitton bag will complete any outfit! Yet, in the dusty (but still super cute) boots of a general contractor, I found a place where my authentic self could thrive amidst concrete and cranes.

We create stories in our minds, envisioning what should be based on what has always been. But when there is no precedent, when the saga is unwritten, that is when the power of belief takes center stage. When people see it, they can believe it, and when they believe it, they can achieve it. I am living proof that you can be both fiercely feminine and formidably skilled in the art of construction.

Often, when I step into meetings with vendors or banking partners, I'm met with incredulous stares. The idea that a woman who loves fashion could also be the mastermind behind large-scale projects seems incongruous to many. I vividly recall one instance at a conservative bank where I presented a proposal for business capital. It feels as if it happened just yesterday—I wore a soft pink double-breasted pantsuit with rhinestone-studded high heels, channeling Reese Witherspoon in "Legally Blonde." Despite the dismissive attitudes of the four men in the room, I remained composed throughout the presentation. In the end, the loan wasn't approved, and I left the meeting feeling deflated. But I wasn't deterred. Their "no" was just a "not yet" to me. I was determined to keep showing up and move on to the next bank until I received the "yes" I needed to achieve my goals.

I must constantly prove myself, validate my knowledge, and demonstrate my capabilities. It can be exhausting, an added weight to the already heavy load of expectations. Yet, it is in these moments that I draw strength from the power of belief—belief in myself and the conviction that I can be whatever I aspire to be. It is a belief that has carried me through the skepticism and the trials, a belief that has transformed every doubt into a steppingstone towards greater heights.

Representation matters because it shatters the preconceived notions of what a general contractor looks like, what she can do, and what she can achieve. It matters because it opens doors for others to walk through to see themselves in roles they may have never imagined possible. It matters because it changes the narrative, not just for me but for the countless women and girls who will follow, who will see in my story a reflection of their own potential.

My story is not just about breaking through glass ceilings; it is about laying down new foundations in which every girl who dreams of commanding construction meetings in her high heels can stride forward without hesitation. It is about building a world where our worth is measured not by the stereotypes we defy but by the authenticity we bring to every beam we raise and every wall we construct.

◆◆◆◆◆◆◆◆◆◆◆◆◆◆◆◆◆◆

PART II

Empowering Women in Male-Dominated Industries

In the architecture of success, every woman is her own architect, curating a blueprint that transforms challenges into growth and potential into power. – Tammie Ross

CHAPTER 4

Curating a Blueprint for Success

◆◆◆◆◆◆◆◆◆◆◆◆◆◆

As I navigated the complex landscape of the construction industry, I recognized the indispensable need for a well-constructed blueprint—a guide to outline the path to success and serve as a roadmap through challenges and opportunities. Having a blueprint for success empowers you to navigate your journey with confidence and purpose.

Establishing goals is akin to laying the foundation for a sturdy structure. Clearly defined and transparent goals act as the pillars that uphold your journey. Recognizing this early on, I understood the significance of setting ambitious yet realistic goals that would inspire me and chart my progress.

For Residence by Ross, I outlined specific targets, detailing the types of projects I aimed to undertake, the financial milestones I wanted to achieve, and the broader impact I envisioned making in the industry. My goals went beyond personal achievements; I aimed to redefine the landscape for women in the construction domain.

Embarking on a career in an industry traditionally dominated by men and setting ambitious goals demands courage and unwavering conviction. Begin by envisioning your long-term aspirations and breaking them down into actionable, attainable milestones. It is essential that your goals reflect your personal ambitions and demonstrate a dedication to reshaping the trajectory for women in your field. Find inspiration in each milestone accomplished, allowing it to propel you toward the next.

Setting a clear, compelling goal mobilizes your focus toward actionable behavior. In essence, goal setting should ignite motivation within you. For instance, consider Joan Doe's goal of saving money to purchase a new house. If her goal is vague, such as wanting "a house in the suburbs," it may not motivate her. However, a specific goal like "save $10,000 by December to buy a house in Eads, Tennessee," provides a clear target, triggering focus and motivating action. Setting a goal directs your attention toward the next steps; it guides you in the right direction and compels your actions to follow suit. As the saying goes, "What you think is who you are; what you do is who you become. Your beliefs determine your actions; your actions determine your destiny."

Witnessing progress is invigorating. Progress fuels momentum, like a snowball growing as it rolls downhill. Momentum is addictive because of the dopamine released in your brain upon achieving a reward. Just like being "in the groove," momentum keeps you going, propelling you forward and fostering a state of mental performance known as flow.

Goal setting helps align your focus with your actions by providing feedback on your progress. Your actions, or lack thereof, offer insights into your values, beliefs, challenges, strengths, and weaknesses. This feedback allows you to make necessary adjustments and realign your focus accordingly.

Perhaps the most significant aspect of goal setting is its role in character-building. Achieving goals builds self-efficacy and shapes you into the type of person who can accomplish goals. Although goal setting is necessary to uncover what you want to accomplish, working toward your goals is where real growth and development occur. Remember, you cannot manage what you do not measure, and you cannot improve what you do not manage. It all begins with goal setting.

Strategic Planning: Paving the Path to Success

With a clear focus on goals, the next critical step is strategic planning. It entails crafting a detailed roadmap that is aimed at seizing opportunities and overcoming potential obstacles. My strategic plan detailed the immediate actions necessary to propel Residence by Ross forward. It also encompassed my long-term vision of establishing a legacy as a nationally recognized builder and industry thought leader. It involved considerations of scalability, diversification, and sustainability. Strategic planning went beyond individual projects; it was an endeavor to leave a permanent mark on the construction industry.

Constructing a strategic plan involves envisioning the immediate steps that must be taken to reach the goal and the broader trajectory of one's career. Identifying pivotal milestones, anticipating challenges, and exploring pathways for expansion are crucial aspects of strategic planning. Seeking guidance from mentors who have navigated similar paths can provide invaluable insights to refine the plan. It is important to remember that strategic planning is an evolving process; remaining open to adaptation as one's career unfolds is essential.

Strategic planning is an ongoing process through which an individual sets their course by engaging all stakeholders to assess current realities and define a vision for the future. It involves examining strengths and weaknesses, managing available resources, and seizing opportunities while anticipating future industry trends. The strategic plan should be a shared document that outlines the organization's purpose, vision, and long-term strategic goals.

These strategic goals inform operational objectives and incremental milestones tied to measurable metrics, ensuring accountability across the organization. The plan should be flexible enough to allow for adjustments based on internal and external factors.

For individuals, strategic planning involves thinking through ways to achieve desired outcomes. It helps individuals grow and achieve goals in a unified direction by working backward from the desired outcome and identifying the steps needed to reach it.

While no plan is foolproof, those who are adept at strategic planning can ensure that their actions align with their desired outcomes. Even when faced with setbacks, their long-term goals serve as a guide to realign their efforts. Envisioning desired future states and devising strategies to turn them into reality enhances an individual's sense of purpose and motivation.

Skill Development:
The Ever-Changing Landscape

In the ever-changing landscape of construction, one thing remains constant: the need for continual skill development. Success in this field demands an ongoing dedication to learning and honing one's abilities. Recognizing this, I embarked on a journey to expand my skill set through various avenues.

From staying abreast of the latest construction technologies to mastering cutting-edge project management techniques, each new skill I acquired added another layer to my expertise. My aim was not just to meet industry standards but to surpass them, positioning Residence by Ross as a leader in innovation and proficiency.

Continuous learning forms the bedrock of success in any industry. It is essential to identify the skills that align with your career goals and invest time in mastering them. Embracing additional certifications and training opportunities is crucial. Engaging with professional organizations, attending workshops, and participating in conferences are effective ways to stay informed about industry trends. By committing to skill development, you can enhance your competencies and challenge gender stereotypes within your field.

In today's rapidly evolving job market, remaining competitive requires a steadfast commitment to continuous learning and upskilling. With the advent of automation and artificial intelligence, traditional job roles are undergoing significant transformations, necessitating a proactive approach to skill enhancement. To thrive in this dynamic environment, professionals must embrace a growth mindset and be adaptable to new technologies and industry trends.

For leaders, fostering a culture of continuous learning within their organizations is paramount. This involves promoting upskilling initiatives, providing access to training programs, and leading by example through their own commitment to personal and professional development. By embracing these strategies, professionals can position themselves for success and remain ahead of the curve in their careers.

Networking: Forging Connections in the Industry

No blueprint is complete without considering connections—the bridges that link us to opportunities, insights, and collaborative ventures. Networking has been an integral part of my journey in the construction sector.

I dedicated significant time and effort to building a strong professional network within the industry. As we were establishing ourselves as builders and forming relationships with vendors and subcontractors, we were fortunate to find individuals who genuinely supported us and helped guide us through the challenges of being new business owners. One person who stands out is Alan Hargett, one of our vendors. He offered to be available for Rod and me whenever we needed him. There were times I would call him on a Sunday evening or send an early morning text, and Alan always responded with positive assurance and valuable guidance. Additionally, we joined organizations like the National Association of Home Builders and the West Tennessee Home Builders Association and made a point to attend networking events.

I also actively sought connections beyond the construction industry, looking for individuals and groups that could offer fresh perspectives and new ideas. For example, I connected with a group of tech entrepreneurs exploring the use of AI in project management. This collaboration introduced us to innovative solutions that improved our project efficiency and accuracy.

These connections opened doors to collaborations and partnerships that transcended traditional norms and enriched my journey unexpectedly.

Networking was not just about expanding my business; it was about contributing to and benefiting from a collective pool of knowledge and experience, creating a supportive community for myself and others. I will delve deeper into the strategies and tactics

I employed to build and nurture my professional network and offer practical insights and actionable advice for cultivating meaningful connections in any industry.

Success in business is not a solitary pursuit. It is a collaborative symphony where goals, strategic planning, skill development, and networking harmonize to create a melody of achievement. Armed with this blueprint, Residence by Ross transcended mere construction—it was tangible evidence of the power of intentional goal setting, strategic foresight, continuous learning, and meaningful connections.

See the appendix for an example for creating your blueprint.

TAKEAWAYS

◆ **Blueprint for Success:** A well-constructed blueprint is crucial for navigating any industry, serving as a guide to outline the path to success and provide direction amid challenges.

◆ **Setting Goals:** Establishing clear, ambitious, and realistic goals is foundational, acting as pillars that uphold the journey and chart progress.

◆ **Empowerment:** Women can empower themselves by creating their own blueprints for success, setting goals that reflect personal ambitions, and a dedication to reshaping the narrative for women in their industry.

◆ **Strategic Planning:** A detailed strategic plan is essential for seizing opportunities, overcoming obstacles, and establishing a legacy.

◆ **Skill Development:** Continuous learning and skill development are imperative to surpass industry standards and position oneself as a leader in innovation and proficiency.

◆ **Networking:** Networking is not merely a tool for business expansion; it is a foundational element that connects individuals to a wealth of opportunities, insights, and collaborative ventures, enriching their professional journey and transcending traditional industry norms.

REFLECTIONS

☐ **Goal Setting:**

▶ What are your long-term aspirations in your field?

▶ How can you break them down into actionable, attainable milestones?

☐ **Strategic Planning:**

▶ How can you craft a detailed roadmap that guides you through the complexities of career progression and business success in your industry?

☐ **Skill Development:**

▶ What are the skills that align with your career goals?

▶ How can you invest time in mastering them?

☐ **Networking:**

▶ How can you build a robust professional network within your industry?

▶ How can you seek connections beyond the boundaries of your industry that offer fresh perspectives and novel ideas?

☐ **Continuous Learning:**

▶ How can you foster a culture of continuous learning and upskilling in your professional journey?

☐ **Collaborative Symphony:**

▶ How can you ensure that your goals, strategic planning, skill development, and networking harmonize to create a melody of achievement in your career?

☐ **Blueprint for Success:**

▶ How can you create your own blueprint for success?

CHAPTER 5

The Transformative Power of a Growth Mindset

◆◆◆◆◆◆◆◆◆◆◆◆◆◆

Our mindset shapes not only our everyday lives but also the world we choose to inhabit. It is the chief architect of our current circumstances and future possibilities, guiding our actions both individually and collectively. If we aspire to alter external aspects of our lives or reconstruct our world, we must be receptive to changing our mindsets.

In her bestselling book *Mindset: The New Psychology of Success,* renowned psychologist and Stanford University professor Carol Dweck explores how our preconceived notions and beliefs about life situations, our perceived talents, and our intelligence can influence our behaviors and reactions. Our mindset can create a self-fulfilling effect on our initial beliefs or biases, as famously encapsulated by Descartes' phrase, "I think, therefore I am." This illustrates how our mindset can influence reality by shaping how we perceive and interact with the world around us.

Dweck conducted extensive research to understand why some individuals succeed while others with similar talents do not. Her studies revealed that mindset plays a pivotal role in this discrepancy. Successful individuals in various fields share common mindset attributes, using their mindset as the foundation for learning, growth, and skill development. Dweck's research identified two distinct perspectives on intelligence and skill development: the fixed mindset and the growth mindset. Understanding these concepts is crucial for unlocking personal potential and fostering a mindset that leads to success.[1]

Fixed Mindset: The Trap of Inflexibility

A fixed mindset is a belief system in which individuals view their talents and skills as innate and unchangeable. People with this mindset believe that their success or failure is predetermined by their natural abilities, leading them to avoid challenges that could reveal their limitations. This avoidance behavior stems from a fear of being judged or exposed as lacking the requisite skills or intelligence. As a result, fixed-mindset individuals often shy away from new experiences, risks, and efforts that could lead to personal growth.

In a fixed mindset, effort is seen as a sign of inadequacy. The belief that talent is static can create resistance to exerting extra effort, limiting personal and professional development. This perspective focuses on appearances and external validation, as fixed mindset individuals are more concerned with how others perceive them. This emphasis on maintaining an image of competence often stifles creativity and innovation, as they avoid situations where they might fail or make mistakes.

A fixed mindset can also impact how people view feedback and criticism. Since they associate their abilities with their inherent worth, they will likely react defensively to criticism, creating a barrier to learning and growth. This defensiveness can prevent them from accepting constructive feedback and using it to improve their skills. As a result, fixed mindset individuals may struggle to progress, reinforcing the cycle of self-imposed limitations.

Breaking free from a fixed mindset requires a shift in perspective, emphasizing growth and learning over static definitions of ability. It involves embracing the idea that talents and skills can be developed through hard work and dedication. This shift encourages individuals to view challenges as opportunities for growth rather than threats to their competence. By accepting that failure is a natural part of learning, they can begin to see setbacks as steppingstones to success.

Growth Mindset:
Embracing Learning and Development

A growth mindset is characterized by the belief that skills and talents can be cultivated through effort and learning. Individuals with this mindset view challenges as chances to grow and embrace the process of improvement. They recognize that success depends on hard work, persistence, and adaptability. Instead of seeking to prove their competence, they focus on developing it, acknowledging that setbacks and mistakes are part of the journey. This perspective fosters resilience, encouraging individuals to persevere despite adversity.

A key aspect of the growth mindset is accepting learning as a continuous journey. People with this mindset are unafraid to explore new areas, acquire new skills, or challenge themselves differently. They view effort as an investment in their development, knowing that each step forward contributes to their long-term success. This proactive attitude towards learning encourages a culture of growth and continual improvement, where the focus is on the journey rather than the immediate outcome.

Growth mindset individuals are more likely to view challenges as opportunities to stretch their abilities and gain valuable experience. They embrace difficulties, understanding that each obstacle is a chance to learn and grow. This perspective leads to greater resilience, enabling them to take risks and pursue their goals with confidence.

A hallmark of the growth mindset is the acceptance of setbacks and mistakes as integral parts of the journey. Individuals with a growth mindset recognize that failure does not define them but provides valuable lessons for improvement. This attitude allows them to analyze their mistakes, extract insights, and use them to guide future actions. By embracing setbacks, they develop a stronger sense of resilience and adaptability, allowing them to navigate the complexities of life with a positive outlook.

Cultivating a Growth Mindset

Cultivating a growth mindset is an ongoing process that requires consistent effort and a willingness to embrace change. It begins with recognizing and challenging the core beliefs that limit personal development. By examining our underlying assumptions, we can uncover the barriers that hold us back and replace them with a more flexible and growth-oriented perspective.

A critical step in cultivating a growth mindset is to seek diverse experiences and engage with people from different backgrounds. This exposure to various viewpoints broadens our understanding of the world and encourages us to reconsider our preconceived notions. It is through these interactions that we can develop empathy, a key component of a growth mindset, allowing us to connect with others and learn from their experiences.

Feedback and constructive criticism play a crucial role in developing a growth mindset. To embrace feedback effectively, it is essential to create an environment where constructive criticism is encouraged and valued. This involves seeking feedback from trusted mentors, colleagues, or peers who can provide honest and objective insights. By actively seeking feedback, we can identify areas for improvement and take concrete steps to address them.

Embracing feedback also involves cultivating a mindset of humility, recognizing that everyone has room for growth and that mistakes are part of the learning process. This mindset encourages us to view feedback not as a threat but as a valuable resource for personal development. By incorporating feedback into our decision-making processes, we can make more informed choices and enhance our overall effectiveness.

The Role of Perseverance and Resilience in Developing a Growth Mindset

Perseverance and resilience are key traits of a growth mindset. Individuals with a growth mindset understand that achieving success requires persistence and determination, even in the face of adversity. This resilience allows them to navigate challenging situations and maintain a positive outlook, knowing that setbacks are temporary.

To develop these traits, it is important to cultivate a mindset that values effort and hard work. This involves setting realistic goals, breaking them down into manageable steps, and celebrating progress along the way. By focusing on the process of growth rather than the end result, we can build the fortitude needed to persist through challenges and setbacks.

Resilience also involves maintaining a sense of purpose and staying focused on long-term goals. This sense of purpose provides the motivation to keep going, even when the journey becomes difficult. It helps us stay grounded and maintain a positive attitude, knowing that each step forward brings us closer to achieving our dreams.

Examples of Mindset in Successful Individuals

Consider the following examples from individuals who embody a growth mindset across various fields:

Amelia Earhart famously stated, "The most difficult thing is the decision to act, the rest is merely tenacity." This perspective highlights the significance of taking action and persisting through challenges, which are key components of a growth mindset.

Michelle Obama encapsulates the growth mindset principle of dedication to effort, stating, "The only limit to the height of your achievements is the reach of your dreams and your willingness to work hard for them." Her statement stresses that success is determined by one's aspirations and effort, rather than fixed abilities.

Dolly Parton also demonstrates a growth mindset with her approach to change. She said, "If you don't like the road you're walking, start paving another one." Dolly's quote underscores the importance of taking control of one's path and making changes to achieve desired outcomes.

Oprah Winfrey once said, "Step out of the history that is holding you back. Step into the new story you are willing to create." This quote reflects a growth mindset by emphasizing the importance of moving beyond past limitations and actively shaping one's future.

These accomplished individuals demonstrated a belief in their potential for growth and the power of effort to shape their outcomes. They focused on their missions and passions rather than solely on external validation. Their successes are the result of a commitment to continuous learning and improvement. They understood that skills and talents could be developed through hard work, and they effectively employed their "Inner CEO" to cultivate a growth mindset.

Our Inner CEO: Managing the Mind

Our inner CEO is the part of our mind that oversees our emotional responses, behaviors, reactions to challenges, and decision-making processes. It plays a pivotal role in determining whether our choices align with our beliefs and emotions, ultimately influencing whether we take positive or negative actions. The inner CEO brings logic to emotional responses, helps prioritize resources, and fosters a growth mindset belief system. As it gains experience and strength, it enhances our ability to believe in ourselves, overcome obstacles, and accomplish our goals.

Think of your brain as a high-performance Formula One race car, with beliefs acting as the drivetrain that provides the power for acceleration. Your inner CEO is the driver of this powerful machine, responsible for steering the vehicle, responding to the track ahead, and adjusting to changing conditions. When engaged effectively, the inner CEO ensures smooth and efficient performance, but when inexperienced or disengaged, it can lead to setbacks or even disasters.

The inner CEO does not just manage your daily operations; it also plays a crucial role in shaping how you respond to adversity and setbacks. This concept is reminiscent of the cherished childhood story *The Little Engine That Could*, which I often read to my young children. It's the story of a small engine tasked with pulling a heavy load over a steep mountain. Despite skepticism from larger engines and the daunting nature of the task, the little engine's simple mantra—"I think I can, I think I can"—drives it to success.

The parallels between the inner CEO and the spirit of the little engine are striking. Just as the inner CEO can guide us to face challenges with confidence and purpose, the little engine's steadfast belief in its abilities propels it forward. The story highlights the transformative power of mindset, illustrating that even the most daunting challenges can be overcome with diligence and a positive attitude.

It is a powerful example of the resilience and determination that reside within us all. It reminds us that in the face of adversity, it is not the size or initial strength that matters most but rather the strength of our convictions and our willingness to persevere. This message aligns with the principles of a growth mindset, encouraging us to approach life with a sense of possibility and to believe in our capacity for growth and achievement. This story, once a treasured part of my children's bedtime routine, continues to inspire me and reinforces my belief in the power of positive thinking and determination.[2]

Unlocking the Transformative Power of a Growth Mindset

A growth mindset has the potential to transform our lives. It allows us to embrace challenges, view setbacks as learning opportunities, and foster resilience in the face of adversity. By developing a growth mindset, we can break through self-imposed limitations and achieve our goals, knowing that our abilities are not fixed but capable of expanding through dedication and effort.

The journey toward a growth mindset is one of continuous learning and development, where each step forward brings us closer to realizing our full potential. By embracing a positive attitude toward learning, implementing feedback, and cultivating resilience, we can navigate the complexities of life with confidence and success.

In the early stages of establishing Residence by Ross, we faced numerous challenges, from securing funding to earning the trust of clients and vendors. One particularly difficult moment came when our initial application for a contractor's license was denied. Instead of seeing this as a failure, I viewed it as an opportunity to learn and improve.

I sought feedback from the licensing board, identified areas for improvement, and worked diligently to enhance our application. This involved refining our business plan, securing stronger references, and ensuring our financial statements were flawless. With each revision, we became more confident and better prepared. Ultimately, our persistence paid off—we were granted the license with a higher monetary limit than we had initially expected.

By embracing a growth mindset, we can unlock our full potential and positively impact the world around us. This journey is driven by a sense of purpose and guided by a commitment to continuous growth, reminding us that with determination and a can-do attitude, anything is possible.

TAKEAWAYS

◆ **Mindset Shapes Reality:** Our mindsets influence our actions and perceptions, shaping our current circumstances and future possibilities.

◆ **Fixed vs. Growth Mindset:** A fixed mindset views talents as static, leading to avoidance of challenges. A growth mindset sees skills as developable through effort, fostering resilience and adaptability.

◆ **Embracing Challenges:** A growth mindset views challenges as opportunities for growth, embracing setbacks as part of the learning process.

◆ **Cultivating Growth:** Developing a growth mindset involves seeking diverse experiences, embracing feedback, and valuing perseverance and resilience.

◆ **Growth Mindset in Action:** Successful individuals like Amelia Earhart, Michelle Obama, Dolly Parton, and Oprah Winfrey exemplify the growth mindset through persistence, effort, preparation, and learning from experiences.

◆ **Inner CEO:** The part of our brain that manages emotional responses, behaviors, and decision-making, helping us align actions with beliefs and fostering a growth mindset.

◆ **Resilience and Determination:** *The Little Engine That Could* illustrates growth mindset principles.

◆ **Transformative Potential:** Embracing a growth mindset allows us to view challenges as opportunities, fostering resilience and continuous learning, ultimately unlocking our full potential.

REFLECTIONS

☐ **Mindset Check:**

▶ How do you perceive your abilities and talents? Are there areas where you tend to have a fixed mindset?

▶ What steps can you take to shift toward a growth mindset, embracing challenges and viewing setbacks as learning opportunities?

☐ **Feedback and Learning:**

▶ How do you react when receiving feedback or criticism? Are you open to constructive input?

▶ How can you create an environment where feedback is encouraged and valued?

☐ **Embrace Setbacks:**

▶ Do you view setbacks as failures or steppingstones? How can you reframe setbacks as part of your growth journey?

▶ What strategies can you use to analyze mistakes and extract valuable insights?

☐ **Cultivate Resilience:**

▶ How do you handle adversity? Do you give up easily or persist despite challenges?

▶ What practices can you adopt to strengthen your resilience and adaptability?

☐ **Inner CEO Management:**

▶ Are you aware of your inner dialogue? Is it fostering a growth mindset or reinforcing limitations?

▶ How can you monitor your self-talk and replace fixed mindset beliefs with growth-oriented thoughts?

☐ **Purpose and Passion:**

▶ What drives you? Are you focused on external validation or your inner mission?

▶ How can you clarify your purpose and align your efforts with intrinsic motivations?

CHAPTER 6

A Multifaceted Approach to Empower Women

◆◆◆◆◆◆◆◆◆◆◆◆◆◆

In the realm of construction, a seismic shift to dismantle entrenched stereotypes and embrace the full spectrum of talent and expertise that women can bring is underway. For far too long, women have been confined to the sidelines, their potential stifled by outdated perceptions and systemic roadblocks. But now, as the industry awakens to the power of diversity and inclusion, a new storyline emerges—one of empowerment, equality, and boundless possibilities. As we embark on this journey to empower women in construction, we are blazing a path toward a more equitable industry defined by limitless potential.

Outdated perceptions and stereotypes have long impeded women from participating in the construction industry. These erroneous beliefs take various forms, ranging from assumptions about physical strength to biases regarding women's leadership capabilities. Women of color face even greater challenges due to the intersecting biases of racism and sexism. Further, stereotypes about women's supposed lack of interest or competence in technical fields compound the barriers they encounter.

In his book, *Think Again: The Power of Knowing What You Don't Know*, Adam Grant advocates for questioning entrenched assumptions, even those widely accepted, to uncover blind spots, gain fresh perspectives, and make more informed decisions. Importantly, Grant highlights the value of openness to changing one's mind based on new information or evidence. Instead of rigidly adhering to outdated perceptions and stereotypes, individuals should actively seek disconfirming evidence that challenges their beliefs or preferences. When industry leaders adopt this approach, they become catalysts for empowering women and driving meaningful change.[1]

Educational initiatives are pivotal in challenging stereotypes and fostering interest in construction careers from an early age. Implementing STEM programs tailored for girls, providing hands-on experiences in construction, and showcasing diverse role models who have excelled in the industry can inspire confidence and ambition. Furthermore, mentorship programs connecting aspiring girls and women with seasoned professionals in construction offer invaluable guidance and support, enabling them to navigate challenges and envision their potential within the field.

When women take on roles traditionally dominated by men, they challenge stereotypes and prove that gender does not determine competence or suitability for a specific job. This shift in perspective stimulates innovation and creativity. Women bring unique perspectives, critical thinking skills, and collaborative approaches to the table, enriching the construction process and contributing to more robust and successful outcomes. Embracing diversity in construction not only benefits women but also fortifies the industry, fostering progress and evolution.

Promoting women's empowerment in the construction industry extends beyond mere equality; it represents an investment in the industry's future. By dismantling barriers and ensuring equal opportunities, we unlock the full spectrum of talent and expertise, thereby securing a dynamic future for construction. Achieving this goal requires collaborative efforts across various sectors. Governments, educational institutions, industry associations, and private organizations must unite to allocate resources, provide educational opportunities, and develop targeted initiatives.

Development Resources for Women in Construction

As the demand for construction rises, more opportunities are emerging for women in the field than ever before. Apprenticeships provide formal training under professional supervision, often leading to full-time positions. In contrast, trade schools offer practical skill development in trades such as carpentry, plumbing, and welding, including exposure to construction CRM software.

- Advancing Opportunities for Women through Apprenticeship
- Apprenticeship.gov
- Introduction to Apprenticeship Workshop | Tradeswomen
- Nontraditional Employment for Women
- Women in Non-Traditional Employment Roles

Numerous online courses, blogs, articles, and publications are available for women interested in entering the construction industry.

- Advancement of Women in Construction (on-demand course) | Lorman (lorman.com)
- Sisters in the Brotherhood (carpenters.org/sisters-in-the-brotherhood)
- Trades Training | Hope Renovations (hoperenovations.org/trades-training)

There are also scholarship and grant opportunities specifically for women in the skilled trades.

- Association of Women Contractors Scholarships
- Jeanette Rankin Foundation Scholar Grants
- The Refrigeration School's Women in Skilled Trades Scholarship
- Women in Apprenticeship and Nontraditional Occupations (WANTO) Grant Program

Resources are available to assist in finding the right program and navigating the licensing process.

- Council for Higher Education Accreditation (CHEA)
- Database of Accredited Postsecondary Institutions and Programs
- General Contractor's License Guide
- Women-Owned Small Business Certification

Various associations offer conferences, events, and online resources for women in the skilled trades.

- Groundbreaking Women in Construction (GWIC) Conference
- Home Builders Institute

- ♦ National Association of Black Women in Construction (NABWIC)
- ♦ National Association of Home Builders (NAHB) Professional Women in Building (PWB)
- ♦ National Association of Women in Construction (NAWIC)
- ♦ Women In Construction Summit

Investing in women's education cultivates a skilled and diverse workforce and fosters a culture of innovation and excellence. This investment yields dividends in the form of a competitive, socially responsible construction industry that benefits society at large.

Building Supportive Networks

Building a supportive network is critical for personal and professional growth, as it provides a foundation of connections, resources, and encouragement to help navigate challenges and pursue goals effectively. In *Networking Like a Pro: Turning Contacts into Connections*, Ivan Misner provides the following key points:

Develop a Networking Mindset: To build supportive networks, adopt a mindset focused on giving and helping others. Embrace the principle of reciprocity by offering support, advice, and resources to your connections without expecting immediate returns. By approaching networking with a genuine desire to contribute to others' success, you can foster a culture of support and collaboration within your network.

Build a Networking Plan: Identify the types of support you need (mentorship, advice, or emotional encouragement) and set goals for expanding your network accordingly. Determine the key individuals or groups that can provide the support you seek and develop strategies for engaging with them effectively.

Make Meaningful Connections: Join organizations where you can connect with like-minded individuals. Actively participate in discussions, offer assistance, and seek opportunities to build relationships based on mutual support and encouragement. Utilize social media platforms and online networking tools to expand your reach and connect with individuals beyond geographical limitations.

Activate the Visibility, Credibility, Profitability (VCP) Process: Increase your visibility within relevant communities by sharing your knowledge, experiences, and insights. As you build credibility through consistent engagement and contributions, you will earn the trust and respect of others, laying the foundation for supportive connections. Ultimately, strive to establish mutually beneficial relationships where support flows freely in both directions.

Observe Networking Etiquette and Best Practices: Maintain professionalism and courtesy in your interactions with others, and always display networking etiquette. Practice active listening, show appreciation for others' contributions, and follow up promptly on commitments or offers of assistance. Lastly, it is important to respect boundaries and preferences to develop relationships built on trust and mutual respect.

By incorporating these key points into your approach to building supportive networks, you can create a robust ecosystem of connections that will uplift and empower you on your journey toward personal and professional fulfillment. Remember, building supportive networks is not just about what you can gain but also about what you can contribute to others' success and well-being. Networking can be a rewarding and enriching experience.[2]

Inspiring the Next Generation

Women in the construction industry have the potential to blaze trails for the next generation by actively participating in outreach programs at schools, community centers, or youth organizations. They can share their experiences and insights and serve as inspiring figures for young girls. By serving as role models and recounting their success stories, women in construction can demonstrate to young girls that they, too, can excel in these fields.

I find immense satisfaction in participating in school career days and leading workshops that inspire young minds about the importance of homeownership. One particularly memorable experience was serving as the keynote speaker at a homebuyer seminar. The seminar aimed to empower attendees by providing the knowledge and tools needed to navigate the home buying process, making it feel less overwhelming and more attainable.

During my presentation, I offered practical advice on becoming a homeowner, stressing the importance of financial planning and the long-term benefits of real estate investment. I covered topics such as budgeting, understanding credit scores, and exploring different mortgage options. I also emphasized the value of working with trusted professionals, like real estate agents and financial advisors, to guide them through the process.

The attendees responded overwhelmingly positively, with many expressing how the information helped demystify the home buying process and gave them the confidence to take their first steps toward homeownership. Witnessing their newfound sense of empowerment was incredibly rewarding. It reinforced the mission Rod and I have always cherished: sharing our knowledge to help others achieve their dreams.

Specialized summer camps tailored for girls, focusing on construction and STEM-related activities, provide invaluable opportunities for hands-on learning and exploration. Participation in such programs enables girls to gain exposure to various facets of the construction industry, ranging from building and design to project management and leadership. These experiences not only nurture practical skills but also foster confidence and empowerment, motivating girls to pursue careers in construction or related fields.

To help young girls envision themselves in roles like architects, engineers, project managers, or industry leaders, women in construction can offer personalized mentorship and guidance aligned with their interests and aspirations. This could involve providing opportunities for job shadowing, internships, apprenticeships, or mentorships. By extending support and encouragement, women in construction can empower young girls to perceive themselves as future leaders and innovators in the industry, contributing to a more diverse and inclusive workforce.

The House That She Built is a captivating children's book that celebrates remarkable women who collaborated to construct a home from the ground up. Through vibrant illustrations and engaging storytelling, young readers are introduced to the diverse talents and roles involved in building a home, from the visionary architect to the skilled roofer. This inspiring story encourages children to recognize their own potential and embrace their unique abilities, sparking curiosity and empowering them to dream big.

There is a pressing need for more books like this one, which captivate young readers' imaginations and inspire them to explore unconventional paths.

Fostering Inclusion and Equity

Verna Myers, a trailblazer in diversity, equity, and inclusion, encapsulates the essence of fostering a truly inclusive environment with her quote: "Diversity is being invited to the party. Inclusion is being asked to dance." Although many diversity initiatives focus on increasing the representation of women in the workforce, true inclusion goes beyond mere numbers. It entails creating an environment where women feel valued, respected, and empowered to contribute their unique perspectives and talents.

In the construction industry, achieving equity means offering women equal opportunities for career advancement, leadership roles, and professional development. This entails addressing systemic barriers such as gender bias, discrimination, and unequal access to resources and opportunities. Additionally, equity involves implementing policies and practices that promote fairness and transparency in hiring, promotion, and compensation, ensuring women are treated equitably at all levels of the organization.

By embracing diversity, nurturing inclusivity, and empowering women through education and mentorship, we break down barriers and pave the way for a more equitable and thriving industry. As we embark on this collective journey, let us continue to champion the pivotal role of women in construction, building a future where every woman's voice is heard, valued, and celebrated in shaping the world around us.

TAKEAWAYS

◆ **Changing Perceptions and Stereotypes:** It is crucial to challenge and change outdated perceptions and stereotypes that impede women's participation in male-dominated industries.

◆ **Educational Opportunities for Skill Development:** Promoting women's empowerment extends beyond mere equality; it represents an investment in the industry's future. We unlock the full spectrum of talent and expertise by dismantling barriers and ensuring equal opportunities.

◆ **Building Supportive Networks:** Building a supportive network is critical for personal and professional growth, providing a foundation of connections, resources, and encouragement.

◆ **Inspiring the Next Generation:** Women have the potential to inspire the next generation by serving as role models and providing mentorship and guidance.

◆ **Fostering Inclusion and Equity:** True inclusion goes beyond mere numbers; it entails creating an environment where women feel valued, respected, and empowered to contribute their unique perspectives and talents.

REFLECTIONS

☐ **Changing Perceptions and Stereotypes:**

▶ What steps can you take to challenge and change the stereotypes in your industry?

☐ **Educational Opportunities for Skill Development:**

▶ How can you leverage educational resources and opportunities to enhance your skills and expertise?

☐ **Building Supportive Networks:**

▶ How can you build a supportive network that provides the connections, resources, and encouragement you need to navigate challenges and pursue your goals?

☐ **Inspiring the Next Generation:**

▶ How can you serve as a role model and provide mentorship and guidance to inspire the next generation of women in your industry?

☐ **Fostering Inclusion and Equity:**

▶ What steps can you take to foster an environment of inclusion and equity in your industry?

☐ **Growth Mindset:**

▶ What can you do to shift toward a growth mindset, embracing challenges and viewing setbacks as opportunities for learning and growth?

☐ **Continuous Learning:**

▶ How can you foster a culture of continuous learning and upskilling in your professional journey?

☐ **Empowering Women:**

▶ How can you contribute to empowering women in your industry?

CHAPTER 7

Constructing a Network: The Influence of Inspirational Figures, Mentors, Allies, and Sponsors

◆◆◆◆◆◆◆◆◆◆◆◆◆

As we embark on the path of personal and professional growth, the profound significance of our social and professional networks is revealed. These networks, intricately woven with mentors, allies, sponsors, and our circle of acquaintances, are vital catalysts for our development, well-being, and success. Each interaction within these networks nurtures the qualities we either possess or strive to develop—positivity, fulfillment, honesty, confidence, empowerment, and ethical integrity. Far from being mere acquaintances, these relationships evolve into deep mentorships that significantly enrich our lives, urging us to transcend our limitations and refine our very essence.

The social sphere we navigate daily is a complex tapestry of interactions and influences, not all of which contribute positively to our journey of self-improvement and fulfillment. Among the myriads of relationships we cultivate, certain ones can deter our personal growth and well-being. Negative influences—individuals who embody skepticism, deceit, or a glaring lack of moral integrity—have the potential to significantly disrupt our path toward self-betterment.

The presence of such individuals in our lives can introduce a climate of doubt and insecurity, steering us away from our goals and dampening our spirit. This realization underscores the critical importance of selective association because the company we keep directly influences our mental and emotional landscape, molding our identity, shaping our beliefs, and, ultimately, determining our destiny.

Recognizing the dynamic power of our social environment compels us to actively curate our interactions. Much like the captain of a ship navigating through turbulent waters, we must be discerning in our engagements, choosing to surround ourselves with individuals whose presence uplifts and aligns with our aspirations. This pursuit goes beyond mere self-interest; it is a shared journey toward mutual growth and enrichment.

When we connect with positive, growth-oriented people, we not only receive support and encouragement, but we also become conduits of motivation and inspiration for others. This mutual exchange of positive energy and support creates a powerful synergy, amplifying the collective development and happiness of our social network. It transforms our circle of acquaintances into a thriving community of mutual advancement, where each member is invested in the growth and success of the others.

Taking charge of our social interactions involves more than distancing ourselves from negative influences; it requires us to actively seek out and foster relationships with individuals who embody the traits we admire and aspire to develop. These individuals could be mentors who guide us with their wisdom, peers who share our ambitions, or even protégés whose growth we wish to support. By intentionally building such connections, we lay the foundation for a supportive environment that not only nurtures our personal growth but also enhances our collective well-being.

This process of selective association and proactive engagement in our social sphere is evidence of the power of community in driving personal and collective advancement. It emphasizes the importance of being mindful of the company we keep, understanding that each interaction can influence our journey. As we navigate the complexities of our social landscape, we can construct a network that mirrors our highest aspirations, a community where support, encouragement, and positive influence flow freely. This curated environment becomes a bastion of mutual growth, where every individual is empowered to pursue their personal development goals, contributing to a culture of collective uplift and prosperity.

Inspirational Figures

In our journey through life and careers, we encounter individuals who leave lasting impressions—people whose wisdom, resilience, and achievements inspire us. Sometimes, we find ourselves admiring those whom we cannot directly access as mentors, allies, or sponsors. Despite this limitation, their influence can still significantly shape our path.

For me, that person was Betty Jotanovic. With an impressive 25-year career in the automotive industry, Betty's story began on the assembly line at Chrysler Motors while she simultaneously pursued a law degree. Her journey was far from easy; she faced personal and professional hurdles. However, her unwavering focus on her goals propelled her forward.

I had the privilege of working with Betty when I served as VP of Risk and Compliance. As the Senior Vice President over Originations, Betty was a formidable presence. Our interactions were impactful, especially when it came to aligning risk management strategies with origination processes. Betty's holistic approach to the industry set her apart. She drew from her diverse experiences, spanning the automotive and finance sectors. From the assembly line to collections, treasury, sales, and operations, she understood the intricate workings of the automotive world. Her resilience and hard work did not go unnoticed; she earned the prestigious title of President of Auto Relationships.

Betty's impact on me transcended mere admiration. Her story reminded me that obstacles can be overcome, and unconventional paths can lead to remarkable destinations. Even without direct access, her example fueled my determination and influenced some of my career choices.

As we navigate our social landscape, let us recognize that even distant figures can profoundly impact us. Their stories, achievements, and unwavering commitment resonate, shaping our beliefs and inspiring our own journeys.

Navigating Professional Growth: The Mentor's Role

Mentors play a crucial role in personal and professional development, providing guidance, support, and insights that help navigate the complexities of one's career. Two remarkable figures—Dr. Virnitia J. Dixon and Tito Williams—shaped my professional journey profoundly.

Dr. Dixon's mentorship went far beyond technical expertise. She helped to transform me into a more strategic leader, visionary, and executor. In my role as Director of Strategic Partnerships, I needed to think strategically, analyze data, and optimize relationships. Dr. Dixon's extensive experience provided insights that extended beyond the immediate challenges of my role. But it wasn't just about numbers and analysis—she taught me the subtle art of influence and navigating the corporate landscape. Knowing when to assert, when to yield, and how to leverage alliances were lessons that made me more resilient and adept at managing complex interpersonal dynamics. Her mentorship helped me see the bigger picture and position myself as a leader capable of driving change and innovation.

Tito Williams' impact was equally profound. He recognized my transferable skills and encouraged me to explore broader horizons within the organization. His guidance shifted my focus from revenue generation to a comprehensive understanding of company dynamics. I learned to assess risks, implement controls, and provide strategic counsel. Tito emphasized the interconnectedness of business functions and how they weave together to form an organization. His mentorship broadened my perspective, enhancing my ability to think strategically about the business as a whole.

Together, Dr. Dixon and Tito Williams offered a balanced mentorship that combined strategic vision with practical execution. They guided me through the complexities of my roles and equipped me with the skills and confidence needed to thrive in a challenging industry. Their influence has been a cornerstone of my professional growth, highlighting the transformative power of mentorship in overcoming barriers and achieving success.

Mentorship begins with a shared vision—a compass pointing toward long-term goals. But it's not just about distant destinations; it's about the journey. As relationships grow, setting guidelines becomes crucial. Trust is the cornerstone. Through open communication and boundaries, mentors and mentees create a productive partnership.

Mentors are not just mere advisors; they become allies and confidantes. Their bespoke support can address skill gaps and leverage a mentee's inherent strengths. It's about personal growth as much as professional development. In mentorship, we find not only just guidance but transformation. Mentors can help mentees form SMART goals—specific, measurable, achievable, relevant, and time-bound—and action plans that transform aspirations into tangible, actionable objectives, providing a clear path forward in the professional sphere.

Paired with constructive feedback, this approach empowers individuals to continuously refine their strategies, adapt to challenges, and pursue their goals with confidence and clarity. This dynamic interplay between goal setting, action planning, and feedback creates a robust framework for professional growth, enabling individuals to navigate their careers with purpose and agility.

Concrete milestones cannot emerge from vague aspirations. The articulation of SMART goals provides clarity. Each goal tailored to context becomes a landmark, guiding progress. But goals alone aren't enough; action plans operationalize them. Breaking down steps, identifying resources, and overcoming obstacles—this methodical planning equips us for the multifaceted professional landscape.

Constructive feedback completes the loop. It's the mirror reflecting progress, strategies, and effectiveness. When offered timely and thoughtfully, it empowers mentees to adapt, evolve, and thrive. Moreover, constructive feedback encourages a dialogue between mentors and mentees. In this space, mentees feel empowered to experiment, take calculated risks, and stretch their capabilities.

The Power of Sponsorship:
Strategic Advocacy for Career Advancement

In *Forget a Mentor, Find a Sponsor*, Sylvia Ann Hewlett explains the nuanced dynamics that distinguish sponsors from mentors in the professional hierarchy. Sponsors play a pivotal role, especially in competitive and often cutthroat workplace environments, where simply having talent and determination might not suffice to ascend the career ladder. Sponsors are seasoned, influential individuals within an organization or industry who go beyond the traditional mentorship role of providing advice and guidance. They actively champion their protégés, using their established credibility and networks to open doors that might otherwise remain closed.[1]

In my own professional journey in the automotive world, I had the distinct honor of being sponsored by Corley Cowan, a leader whose guidance and allyship were unparalleled. I didn't have to ask Corley for sponsorship; it was just in his nature to give it organically. He respected hard work and recognized the efforts of those who worked for him. Corley was the best leader I have ever had the privilege to work for. His leadership style was inspiring, and his unwavering belief in my abilities was a significant confidence booster. He advocated for me to oversee major strategic partners, a responsibility of immense magnitude. Ensuring that senior leaders recognized my efforts, Corley's faith in me was steadfast. He made it a point to ensure that the CEO and President knew that I was instrumental to his team's success. His sponsorship was a testament to his leadership, and his influence was instrumental in my career advancement.

A sponsor's endorsement can position a protégé to be viewed as an asset in the eyes of upper management and key decision-makers. This is not merely about informal recommendations; sponsors strategically place their protégés in projects and roles that suit their skillset and provide visibility and opportunities for substantial impact. By aligning the protégé's aspirations with organizational needs, sponsors ensure that their protégés are not just participants but central figures in high-profile initiatives.

Sponsors' active advocacy can dramatically alter a protégé's career trajectory. Sponsors invest in their protégés, seeing their success as a mutual benefit—a reflection of their judgment and an extension of their legacy. This investment goes beyond mere guidance, encompassing a willingness to stake their reputation on the protégé's performance. Such sponsorship is particularly invaluable in navigating the implicit biases and systemic barriers that might limit access to opportunities for women, minorities, and other underrepresented groups in the workplace.

Furthermore, sponsorship transcends the boundaries of individual projects or roles. Sponsors provide a sustained support system that propels the protégé through various stages of their career progression. This might include advocating for their promotions, inclusion in strategic meetings, and connections with other influential figures within and beyond the organization. Through this comprehensive support, sponsors facilitate professional advancement and the development of leadership capabilities and a broader strategic vision.

The impact of sponsorship on professional growth is substantial and multifaceted. Protégés benefit from accelerated career progression, enhanced visibility, and access to networks that might have been inaccessible otherwise. They acquire strategic allies who provide critical feedback and support and encourage risk-taking during pivotal moments. For the sponsor, the relationship offers the satisfaction of cultivating talent and influencing the next generation of leaders, thereby contributing to a legacy of mentorship and leadership within the organization.

In essence, the concept of sponsorship Hewlett details reveals a dynamic and proactive approach to career advancement, where the active support of influential advocates opens a realm of opportunities for emerging talents. This form of sponsorship is a testament to the power of strategic advocacy in breaking barriers and accelerating professional growth, establishing it as an indispensable catalyst for those seeking to achieve leadership roles and leave a significant mark in their professional fields.

Embracing Allyship:
A Commitment to Equity and Inclusion

In *Better Allies: Everyday Actions to Create Inclusive, Engaging Workplaces*, Karen Catlin delves into the concept of allyship with a focus that is both profound and actionable, illuminating the pathways through which individuals can contribute to creating more equitable professional environments. Allyship is not a passive endorsement of diversity and inclusion principles but an active, ongoing commitment to recognize, understand, and dismantle the systemic inequalities that permeate professional spaces. Allies understand that to foster true inclusivity and equity, it is imperative to confront and challenge the entrenched norms, practices, and barriers that persistently hinder the progress of marginalized groups.[2]

Allyship involves a conscious effort to educate oneself about the diverse experiences of marginalized groups, acknowledging that these experiences are often complex and multifaceted. This education is not a superficial undertaking but a deep, reflective process that involves listening to these voices, seeking out their stories, and understanding the historical and social contexts that shape their professional and personal lives. Allies leverage their positions of privilege—acknowledging that privilege varies widely in context and degree—to advocate for systemic change.

One of the critical actions of allies is to amplify voices that are often silenced or overlooked. This means not only advocating for the inclusion of these voices in decision-making processes and discussions but also recognizing and challenging any discriminatory behaviors or policies that may silence them. Allies actively seek ways to support diversity initiatives, whether by sponsoring events, participating in or facilitating training sessions, or simply by being mindful of language and communication styles.

Moreover, effective allyship extends beyond the confines of the workplace. Allies recognize that the attitudes, biases, and practices within professional environments reflect broader societal dynamics. This dual approach ensures that the push for change is comprehensive and addresses both the symptoms and root causes of inequality and discrimination.

A prime example of effective allyship is demonstrated by Mahesh Aditya, who served as CEO during my tenure in the world of risk and compliance. During the early days of the COVID-19 pandemic in March 2020, I was among the first at our company to contract the virus. Mahesh's response was exemplary; he ensured that I received the necessary support and accommodations to recover fully. His actions went beyond mere compliance with health guidelines; he actively fostered a culture of empathy and understanding within the organization. By demonstrating genuine concern, Mahesh set a powerful example of leadership and allyship that resonated with me and throughout the company.

In addition to this, Mahesh took the time to have listening sessions with every department within the company. He didn't assign one of his direct reports to be his proxy; he led these discussions himself. This hands-on approach created a culture of belonging.

The impact of such allyship is profound. By challenging the status quo and advocating for all-encompassing practices, allies contribute to a shift in organizational culture—one where every individual, regardless of their background or identity, feels valued, respected, and integral to the organization's collective mission. This cultural shift enhances the workplace environment for everyone and enriches the organization's ability to innovate, solve problems, and meet the needs of a wide-ranging clientele.

In essence, the journey toward becoming a better ally, as Catlin details, is a commitment to lifelong learning, advocacy, and action. It is about recognizing that true allyship requires more than just good intentions; it necessitates a willingness to act, make mistakes, learn from mistakes, and persist in the effort to contribute to a more equitable world. Through such dedicated allyship, individuals can play a crucial role in transforming professional spaces into environments where diversity is celebrated, equity is achieved, and every voice is heard.

Our journey toward personal growth and professional achievement is deeply influenced by the company we keep. By judiciously selecting mentors for guidance, sponsors for advocacy, and allies for support, we enrich our personal development and reap the benefits of a more supportive professional environment. This synergistic relationship between mentors, sponsors, and allies creates a powerful dynamic that propels both individuals and communities toward unparalleled heights of fulfillment and success. Embracing these relationships allows us to navigate the complexities of our careers with wisdom, support, and advocacy, setting the stage for a legacy of achievement and meaningful change.

TAKEAWAYS

◆ **The Impact of Social Influences:** Social and professional networks can significantly influence personal and professional growth. The company we keep can nurture our positive qualities or introduce doubt and insecurity. Therefore, it is crucial to forge connections with positive, like-minded individuals and organizations.

◆ **Navigating Professional Growth (The Mentor's Role):** Mentors provide a safe space for expressing fears and ambitions, setting SMART goals, developing action plans, and providing constructive feedback. Mentorship is a valuable tool for personal growth and professional development.

◆ **The Power of Sponsorship (Strategic Advocacy for Career Advancement):** Sponsors are influential individuals who actively champion their protégés. They use their credibility and networks to open doors and place their protégés in high-profile initiatives. This active advocacy can dramatically alter a protégé's career trajectory, especially in navigating implicit biases and systemic barriers.

◆ **Embracing Allyship (A Commitment to Equity and Inclusion):** Allyship is an active commitment to recognize, understand, and dismantle systemic inequalities. Allies understand the diverse experiences of marginalized groups and advocate for systemic change. They amplify voices often silenced or overlooked and contribute to a shift in organizational culture where diversity is valued.

REFLECTIONS

☐ **Social Influences:**

- ▶ Reflect on your current social and professional networks. How do these relationships influence your personal and professional growth?

- ▶ How can you curate your interactions to foster mutual growth and enrichment?

☐ **Mentor's Role:**

- ▶ Do you have a mentor? If not, what steps can you take to find a mentor who aligns with your professional goals and aspirations?

- ▶ How can you leverage mentorship to set SMART goals and develop action plans?

☐ **Power of Sponsorship:**

- ▶ How can you find sponsors within your industry or organization?

- ▶ What steps can you take to demonstrate your potential and attract sponsorship?

☐ **Allyship:**

- ▶ How can you act as an ally within your professional environment?

- ▶ What steps can you take to promote diversity, equity, and inclusion in your workplace?

☐ **Personal Growth:**

- ▶ How can you leverage relationships with mentors, sponsors, and allies to facilitate personal and professional growth?

☐ **Professional Achievement:**

- ▶ How can you contribute to a more inclusive, diverse, and supportive professional environment through interactions with mentors, sponsors, and allies?

☐ **Legacy of Achievement:**

- ▶ How can you use your relationships with mentors, allies, and sponsors to leave a significant mark in your professional field?

- ▶ How can these relationships help you set the stage for a legacy of achievement and systemic change?

CHAPTER 8

Navigating Imposter Syndrome, Sexism, and Microaggressions

◆◆◆◆◆◆◆◆◆◆◆◆◆◆

Sexism, microaggressions, and imposter syndrome represent a complex web of challenges that disproportionately affect women in male-dominated industries. These interconnected issues can create significant barriers to career advancement, undermine mental health, and diminish workplace satisfaction. Understanding their impact is crucial for addressing the underlying causes and fostering an environment where all employees can thrive. This chapter explores these challenges in depth, examining their roots, effects, and strategies to overcome them. It also highlights practical approaches to promoting a more inclusive workplace, where equality and respect are not just ideals but tangible realities.

Imposter syndrome is a psychological phenomenon that plagues even the most accomplished individuals. Despite their achievements, they harbor an irrational fear of being exposed as frauds. For women in male-dominated industries, imposter syndrome is particularly prevalent. The pressure to prove oneself can lead to a cycle of self-doubt, overwork, and burnout. A recent KPMG study revealed that 75% of female executives experience imposter syndrome at some point in their careers.[1] Imposter syndrome can manifest in several ways, often revealing itself through thoughts, behaviors, and emotions. Common manifestations include the following:

Self-Doubt: A constant feeling of not being good enough, even in the face of tangible achievements. Individuals may question their skills, intelligence, or qualifications, attributing success to luck or external factors.

Perfectionism: Imposter syndrome can drive individuals to strive for perfection in all tasks, leading to overwork and burnout. The fear of failure or making mistakes can result in excessive scrutiny of one's own work.

Discounting Achievements: Those with imposter syndrome often downplay their successes, avoiding recognition and attributing accomplishments to factors other than their own abilities.

Comparisons: A tendency to compare oneself to others, often leading to feelings of inadequacy when viewing colleagues' achievements or progress.

Fear of Exposure: A pervasive fear of being "found out" or exposed as a fraud, causing anxiety and reluctance to take on new challenges.

The effects of imposter syndrome can extend beyond the individual, impacting career progression and personal well-being. Individuals may hesitate to pursue promotions, leadership roles, or challenging projects, fearing they lack the skills or knowledge to succeed. This reluctance can hinder career growth and limit opportunities.

The constant pressure to prove oneself and fear of failure can lead to diminished job satisfaction, making work a source of stress rather than fulfillment. Persistent self-doubt and anxiety can contribute to stress, depression, and other mental health issues. The pressure to meet lofty expectations can be overwhelming, affecting work-life balance.

Overcoming imposter syndrome involves a shift in perspective and a commitment to changing thought patterns. Strategies to address this challenge include the following:

Acknowledge Achievements: Recognizing and celebrating successes, regardless of their size, helps counteract the tendency to discount accomplishments. Keeping a record of achievements can serve as a reminder of one's capabilities.

Seek Support and Mentorship: Building a network of supportive colleagues, mentors, or peers provides external validation and encouragement. Mentors can offer guidance and share their own experiences with imposter syndrome, helping to normalize the struggle.

Practice Positive Self-Talk: Replacing negative, self-critical thoughts with positive affirmations can help shift the internal narrative. This practice fosters a more compassionate approach to one's own abilities and achievements.

Embrace Imperfection: Accepting that mistakes are part of growth allows for a more balanced perspective on success. This approach reduces the pressure to be perfect and encourages a growth mindset.

Set Realistic Goals: Establishing achievable goals and breaking them into manageable steps can help reduce the overwhelm of imposter syndrome. Celebrating each milestone reinforces a sense of progress.

Professional Development: Engaging in continuous learning and skill development builds confidence and demonstrates a commitment to personal growth. This can counter the belief that one is not qualified or lacks expertise.

Organizations play a crucial role in addressing imposter syndrome by fostering a supportive and inclusive workplace culture. Key actions include the following strategies:

Promote Diversity and Inclusion: A diverse workforce helps create an environment where different perspectives are valued, reducing the feeling of isolation that imposter syndrome can cause.

Encourage Open Communication: Providing a safe space for employees to discuss their experiences and seek support helps break down the stigma surrounding imposter syndrome.

Recognize and Reward Achievements: Regularly acknowledging employees' accomplishments and contributions reinforces their value and counteracts the tendency to discount successes.

By adopting these strategies, individuals and organizations can work together to overcome imposter syndrome, allowing employees to thrive and achieve their full potential without the burden of constant self-doubt and fear of failure.

Overcoming Imposter Syndrome:
A Personal Journey

In my journey to become a general contractor, I grappled with imposter syndrome. For example, during the International Builders' Show®, my first major industry conference, I found myself surrounded by seasoned professionals discussing complex projects and innovative techniques. Despite my qualifications, I felt like an outsider, questioning whether I truly belonged in such esteemed company. A similar sense of inadequacy had driven me to go above and beyond to even start my construction journey, earning my MBA in project management and obtaining a Six Sigma certification. This pursuit of perfection was exhausting and delayed the opening of my business, as I felt I had to wait until I exceeded expectations to start.

In my journey to overcome imposter syndrome, I found practicing positive self-talk and setting SMART goals particularly helpful. I replaced negative thoughts with positive affirmations, reminding myself of my qualifications and the hard work I had put into my career. Some affirmations that resonated with me included: "I am capable and deserving of my success," and "My skills and dedication make me a valuable asset to any project." This helped me foster a more compassionate approach to my own abilities and achievements.

Setting SMART goals was another crucial step for me. Instead of striving for perfection, I started to set achievable goals and celebrated each milestone, no matter how small. For instance, one of my initial goals was to successfully complete a small residential project within a set budget and timeline. Achieving this goal not only boosted my confidence but also demonstrated my capability to manage larger projects. This practice reduced the overwhelm of imposter syndrome and reinforced a sense of progress and accomplishment within me.

Overcoming imposter syndrome is an ongoing process. Utilizing the strategies in this chapter has been instrumental in helping me manage self-doubt and build confidence in my abilities.

Identifying and Addressing Sexism

Sexual harassment is a form of sexism that affects approximately 50% of women in all workplaces. Women who work in male-dominated occupations may be more susceptible to sexual harassment than those who work in non-male-dominated occupations."[2] Sexism encompasses discriminatory practices and harmful stereotypes based on gender, resulting in unequal treatment and limited opportunities for women. Sexism can manifest in various ways, presenting significant challenges for women seeking career growth and fair treatment. Gender pay gaps, lack of representation in leadership, workplace harassment, and the perpetuation of gender norms contribute to a hostile work environment.

Sexual harassment encompasses a range of unwanted behaviors, including verbal remarks, physical advances, and inappropriate gestures. It can create a toxic work environment where women feel unsafe, uncomfortable, or undervalued. Women may be outnumbered by male colleagues, reducing their support system and increasing the likelihood of harassment. The imbalance of power can make it difficult for women to report harassment or seek recourse. A workplace culture that tolerates or dismisses sexist behavior can encourage sexual harassment and discrimination.

Sexism often involves discriminatory practices, harmful stereotypes, and a lack of equal opportunities for women. It manifests in numerous ways, affecting women's career progression and workplace satisfaction. Women are frequently paid less than their male counterparts, even with similar qualifications and experience. This discrepancy reflects underlying gender bias and reinforces unequal treatment.

A lack of women in leadership positions perpetuates a male-centric culture and limits mentorship and role models for aspiring female leaders. Sexist attitudes often stem from traditional gender roles, leading to the assumption that women are less capable in technical or leadership positions. This can result in women being assigned fewer challenging tasks or being excluded from important projects.

Sexual harassment and sexism contribute to stress, anxiety, and other mental health issues. The constant threat of harassment or discrimination can lead to increased absenteeism and burnout. A hostile work environment affects job satisfaction and can lead to higher turnover rates among women, further skewing gender representation.

Combatting sexism and sexual harassment requires a proactive approach and commitment to creating a safe and inclusive workplace. Organizations should establish clear policies that define and prohibit sexual harassment, with procedures for reporting and addressing complaints. Ensuring these policies are enforced is crucial. Encouraging a diverse workforce, including women in leadership roles, helps create a more balanced workplace culture that does not tolerate discrimination.

Conducting regular training on sexual harassment and sexism raises awareness and promotes respectful behavior. Education about unconscious bias and gender stereotypes helps prevent discriminatory practices. Creating a safe environment for reporting harassment is essential. Organizations should offer support resources, such as employee assistance programs, and ensure that reporting harassment does not lead to retaliation.

Establishing mentorship programs and support networks for women provides a community for guidance and solidarity. These networks can help women navigate workplace challenges and build resilience. Leaders and managers should be accountable for creating a respectful workplace. This includes actively addressing sexist behavior and promoting a culture of inclusion.

By addressing sexism and sexual harassment, organizations can create a more equitable workplace where women can thrive without fear of discrimination or harassment. These strategies foster a positive work environment that encourages career growth and fair treatment, contributing to a more inclusive and successful industry.

Microaggressions: Recognizing and Combating Subtle Bias

Microaggressions are subtle acts or comments that convey hostile or negative messages to marginalized groups. These microaggressions can significantly impact women, reinforcing gender stereotypes and contributing to a workplace culture that is unwelcoming and discriminatory.

Microaggressions are often rooted in implicit biases and reflect societal stereotypes. They can take various forms, including verbal remarks, behavioral patterns, or environmental cues, and can have a profound impact on those targeted. Microaggressions can make individuals feel undervalued or dismissed, contributing to a sense of not belonging in the workplace. Subtle comments that reinforce gender stereotypes can perpetuate discrimination, suggesting that women are less capable or suited for certain roles. They can isolate individuals from critical workplace networks and decision-making processes, limiting their career advancement.

The childhood adage, "Sticks and stones may break my bones, but words will never hurt me," expresses a false belief that words are harmless, small, trivial, and insignificant. "Research is clear about the impact innocuous statements can have on one's physical and mental health, especially over the course of an entire career: increased rates of depression, prolonged stress, and trauma, physical concerns like headaches, high blood pressure, and difficulties with sleep. Microaggressions can negatively impact careers as they are related to increased burnout and less job satisfaction and require significant cognitive and emotional resources to recover from them."[3]

Microaggressions can also hinder professional growth and advancement. Constant exposure to microaggressions can undermine self-confidence, leading to imposter syndrome and reluctance to take on leadership roles. A hostile work environment affects job satisfaction, resulting in lower productivity and higher turnover rates among women. Microaggressions can restrict access to career opportunities, mentorship, and critical projects, limiting the ability to advance.

To combat microaggressions, workplaces must adopt a comprehensive approach that addresses the root causes and creates a more inclusive environment. Raising awareness about microaggressions and their impact helps create a workplace culture that does not tolerate discriminatory behavior. Training on implicit bias and diversity promotes a more respectful environment. Encouraging open discussions about microaggressions allows employees to share their experiences and seek support. This approach fosters a culture of accountability and encourages allies to stand against discriminatory behavior.

Building support networks for women provides a community for guidance and mentorship. These networks offer a safe space to discuss microaggressions and share coping strategies. Leaders and managers must be accountable for addressing microaggressions and promoting a culture of inclusion. This requires clear policies and a commitment to diversity at all levels of the organization. Providing resources for mental health and stress management can help mitigate the impact of microaggressions. Employee assistance programs and counseling services offer valuable support.

By implementing these strategies, workplaces can reduce the prevalence of microaggressions and create a more inclusive and equitable environment. Addressing microaggressions benefits not only the individuals targeted but also the organization, leading to a more harmonious and productive workplace culture.

My Personal Experience with Microaggressions

I have faced my share of microaggressions. Comments such as "You're too pretty to work in construction," or "Your husband is the real builder, isn't he?" or "You're just the face of the company, you can't be the general contractor," have been directed at me. Again, I am a self-proclaimed "girlie girl," and I refuse to change how I dress to appear to be a "real builder." For instance, during a project kickoff meeting, I arrived in a tailored blazer dress and fabulous heels, ready to discuss the project details. As I introduced myself as the general contractor, I noticed a few raised eyebrows and overheard someone whisper, "She doesn't look like she belongs on a construction site." Despite these dismissive comments, I confidently presented my plans and demonstrated my expertise, ultimately earning their respect through my professionalism and knowledge.

Although upsetting, I address these microaggressions directly. When someone questions my role, I confidently respond by highlighting my qualifications and achievements. For example, when someone once said, "You're just the face of the company; you can't be the general contractor," I replied, "Actually, I am the general contractor, and I've successfully managed multiple high-profile projects, including a recent home build in Eads." This approach not only asserts my competence but also educates others about my expertise.

My husband also addresses these comments by standing up for me and reinforcing my role and expertise in the industry. Most importantly, I consistently bring my authentic self to every event I attend. I refuse to let microaggressions change who I am or how I present myself.

Creating a workplace that proactively addresses sexism and microaggressions requires a holistic approach. Through inclusive policies, assertiveness training, fostering support networks, and promoting diversity in leadership, organizations can break down barriers and create a safe, equitable work environment. Addressing these issues in the workplace paves the way for professional success and contributes to employee happiness and fulfillment. Embracing and celebrating your achievements, no matter how small, is key to building a foundation of self-respect and resilience and breaking free of imposter syndrome.

TAKEAWAYS

◆ **Understanding Imposter Syndrome:** Overcoming imposter syndrome involves acknowledging achievements, seeking support and mentorship, practicing positive self-talk, embracing imperfection, setting realistic goals, and engaging in professional development.

◆ **Identifying and Addressing Sexism:** Addressing sexism involves clear anti-harassment policies, promoting diversity and inclusion, training and education, encouraging reporting and support, mentorship and support networks, and holding leadership accountable.

◆ **Recognizing and Combating Microaggressions:** Addressing microaggressions involves raising awareness and education, encouraging open communication, building support networks and mentorship, leadership accountability, and employee well-being programs.

REFLECTIONS

☐ **Imposter Syndrome:**

▶ Reflect on your experiences with imposter syndrome. How has it impacted your career progression and personal well-being?

▶ What strategies can you implement to overcome it?

☐ **Sexism:**

▶ Have you experienced sexism in your workplace? How has it impacted your career growth and job satisfaction?

▶ What steps can you take to address sexism in your workplace?

☐ **Microaggressions:**

▶ Have you encountered microaggressions in your professional environment? How have they impacted your confidence and job satisfaction?

▶ What strategies can you use to combat subtle bias?

☐ **Creating a Supportive Work Environment:**

▶ What steps can your organization take to create a more supportive and inclusive work environment?

▶ How can you contribute to this effort?

☐ **Personal Growth:**

▶ How can you leverage your experiences and relationships to facilitate your personal and professional growth?

☐ **Professional Achievement:**

▶ How can you contribute to a more inclusive, diverse, and supportive professional environment through your interactions and actions?

☐ **Legacy of Achievement:**

▶ How can you use your experiences and insights to leave a significant mark in your professional field?

▶ How can these experiences help you set the stage for a legacy of achievement and systemic change?

CHAPTER 9

Unlocking Success Through Emotional Intelligence

◆◆◆◆◆◆◆◆◆◆◆◆◆◆

In today's dynamic business world, characterized by relentless competition and constant change, emotional intelligence (EI) has emerged as a fundamental skill that is essential for achieving success. Unlike technical prowess or academic knowledge, EI revolves around the capacity to understand and regulate one's emotions. The ability to cultivate EI is increasingly vital as workplaces become more diverse and demand adaptability and flexibility.

In male-dominated industries, EI is more than a mere professional asset; it is a transformative tool. Mastery of EI empowers women to navigate intricate workplace dynamics, dismantle gender-based barriers, and cultivate a more equitable environment. It serves as a gateway to leadership roles, fosters collaboration, and challenges conventional hierarchies, thereby contributing to a more balanced representation of women across various industries.

Emotional intelligence encompasses a broad array of skills that enable individuals to manage emotions and engage with others meaningfully. These skills are indispensable in professional environments where interpersonal interactions, teamwork, and effective communication are pivotal to success. Travis Bradberry and Jean Greaves, in their book *Emotional Intelligence 2.0,* outline four key components of EI: self-awareness, self-regulation, empathy, and social skills.[1]

Self-awareness forms the bedrock of EI. It entails recognizing one's emotions and comprehending their influence on thoughts, actions, and decision-making processes. Self-awareness fosters better decision-making, enhanced relationships, and the ability to maintain authenticity. Practices such as journaling, meditation, and seeking feedback aid in nurturing self-awareness.

Self-regulation builds upon self-awareness by focusing on constructive management of emotions. It involves maintaining composure in stressful situations, refraining from impulsive reactions, and responding thoughtfully to criticism. Self-regulation enables individuals to navigate high-pressure scenarios with poise, thereby fostering more harmonious relationships. Techniques like breathing exercises and mindfulness bolster self-regulation.

Empathy denotes the capacity to comprehend and connect with others' emotions, fostering trust and fortifying relationships—a cornerstone of a collaborative work environment. Empathy entails recognizing others' perspectives and demonstrating genuine concern. Active listening and displaying interest in others' experiences are pivotal in honing empathy.

Social skills encompass an array of abilities facilitating effective communication, conflict resolution, and collaboration—crucial for cultivating robust relationships and fostering teamwork, especially in complex workplace environments. Strong social skills enable individuals to forge connections and resolve conflicts constructively. Active listening, clear communication, and adaptability are focal points for enhancing social skills.

The Significance of Emotional Intelligence for Women

EI exerts a profound influence on personal and professional growth, and it is a valuable tool for women to surmount obstacles, cope with stress, and maintain focus amidst adversity. Through self-awareness and self-regulation, women can rebound from setbacks and stay resolute in pursuing their goals.

EI is indispensable for navigating intricate power dynamics and fostering robust interpersonal relationships. It empowers women to adeptly manage conflicts and cultivate rapport with colleagues and stakeholders, fostering a collaborative ambiance. This empathetic approach not only enhances workplace relationships but also engenders a supportive network crucial for career advancement.

EI also engenders resilience and self-assurance, enabling women to assert themselves and confidently champion their ideas—essential attributes in environments rife with stereotypes and discrimination. By nurturing self-awareness, women can overcome self-doubt and communicate assertively, ensuring their voices resonate in decision-making processes.

EI is a hallmark of effective leaders. Women endowed with high EI can inspire trust, galvanize teams, and cultivate a positive workplace culture. Their ability to manage emotions and resolve conflicts fosters sustainable success, enabling them to effect substantial change within their domains.

Intersectionality and Emotional Intelligence

Intersectionality is how various aspects of identity, such as race, ethnicity, gender, sexual orientation, and socioeconomic status, intersect and shape individuals' experiences and opportunities. It can contribute to unequal outcomes in ways that cannot be attributed to one aspect of a person's identity. For example, I am not only a woman, but I am also African-American. Therefore, I am navigating the intersectionality of gender and race.

In the context of EI, intersectionality underscores the importance of recognizing and addressing the unique challenges and barriers faced by individuals with multiple marginalized identities. These intersecting identities can influence how emotions are perceived and managed, as well as the opportunities for advancement and recognition available to them. According to the World Economic Forum, "in 2020, while white women in the US earn 81 cents for every dollar a white man earns, the same figure for African American and Hispanic women is 75 cents. Read another way, while white women will reach gender parity with men in the US in 2059, the data shows that for African American women this date is 2130, and 2224 for Hispanic women."[2]

Additionally, "research shows that Black women have less access to training, have received less mentorship and sponsorship, and have less frequent opportunities to interact with senior leaders. As a result, while only 21% of C-suite leaders in the US are women, only 4% are women of color, and only 1% are Black women."[3] Acknowledging the dynamics of intersectionality is the first step in employing EI. In this example, companies can assist in addressing this disparity by proactively taking to the time to "collect and analyze data on pay and employee engagement, separating out variables of race, gender, sexual orientation, or physical ability" and create systemic changes within their organization.

Furthermore, the intersectionality of EI emphasizes the need for inclusive approaches to EI training and development. Programs and interventions aimed at enhancing EI should consider the diverse backgrounds and experiences of participants, providing tailored strategies and support to address the specific challenges they may face. By acknowledging and valuing the intersectionality of EI, organizations can foster a more inclusive and equitable workplace culture where all individuals can thrive.

My Experience with Intersectionality and Emotional Intelligence

As an African-American woman who has primarily worked in male-dominated industries, I have found myself at the intersection of multiple identities. I have often had to navigate the stereotype of the "angry Black woman," especially during difficult conversations. For example, during a heated discussion about project deadlines, I firmly voiced my concerns about the timelines not being followed. Despite my professional tone and valid points, a colleague responded with, "You don't have to get so angry about it," implying that my assertiveness was unwarranted and aggressive.

Despite these challenges, I have been wrongly labeled as aggressive and intimidating, not because of my actions or words, but because of ingrained stereotypes. I strive to communicate my thoughts and ideas clearly and respectfully, standing firm in my convictions while also being open to the perspectives of others. Being called an "angry Black woman" is a clear misunderstanding and misinterpretation of my assertiveness and confidence.

In these situations, I employed emotional intelligence by recognizing and understanding these biases and managing my emotions accordingly. I draw strength from the words of Former First Lady Michelle Obama, "When they go low, we go high." I have often had to bear the brunt of heated conversations and maintain my composure to dispel the stereotype of the "angry Black woman."

By employing emotional intelligence, I have been able to navigate these challenging situations, manage my emotions effectively, and maintain my professionalism. This has not only helped me to overcome these stereotypes but also to foster a more inclusive and respectful workplace culture.

Strategies for Enhancing Emotional Intelligence

In the book *Emotional Intelligence Habits: How to Manage Your Emotions, Improve Your Relationships, and Increase Your EQ*, Travis Bradberry underscores the integration of EI principles into daily life as the pathway to heightened emotional intelligence. This entails continual practice rather than a one-time effort, necessitating a flexible mindset. To cultivate EI habits, individuals must consciously infuse emotional intelligence into their daily routines and foster an environment conducive to emotional growth. This process of embedding EI into everyday activities facilitates the enhancement of interpersonal skills and more effective stress management.[4]

To apply EI habits, start by identifying moments in daily life conducive to practicing self-awareness and self-regulation. This might occur during stressful work situations, interactions with colleagues or clients, or even during personal downtime. Techniques such as mindfulness, meditation, and deep breathing exercises aid in emotion management and stress reduction, enabling individuals to remain grounded, discern emotional triggers, and respond thoughtfully to challenging circumstances.

Creating a supportive environment is pivotal in developing EI habits. This involves nurturing a culture that champions open communication and emotional development. In professional contexts, this could entail advocating for regular feedback sessions, engaging in team-building activities, or fostering an inclusive atmosphere where all individuals feel valued. A supportive setting facilitates consistent practice of EI habits, reinforcing positive outcomes at both individual and collective levels.

Feedback and reflection are integral components of building EI habits. Soliciting feedback from colleagues, mentors, or peers offers external perspectives on behavior and emotional responses, facilitating identification of areas for improvement and comprehension of how one is perceived by others. Embracing constructive criticism and leveraging it to enhance emotional intelligence can markedly accelerate personal growth.

Reflection, an internal process involving contemplation of one's actions, reactions, and emotional state, is paramount. Allocating time for introspection, perhaps through journaling, enables individuals to track progress and discern patterns in behavior. Regular reflection facilitates a deeper understanding of strengths and weaknesses, fostering intentional development of EI habits.

Technology and Emotional Intelligence

Technology significantly shapes how we perceive, express, and manage emotions in today's digital age. The advent of digital communication platforms has transformed the way we interact with others, presenting both opportunities and challenges for EI development.

On one hand, digital communication tools such as email, social media, and instant messaging have expanded our ability to connect with others across distances and cultures. However, the absence of non-verbal cues in digital communication can pose challenges for accurately interpreting and responding to emotions, potentially leading to misunderstandings and conflicts.

Moreover, the rise of artificial intelligence (AI) emotional intelligence tools presents both promise and peril. On the one hand, these tools hold the potential to augment human capabilities in understanding and managing emotions, offering insights and feedback that can enhance EI development. For example, AI-powered chatbots and virtual assistants can provide personalized support and guidance for improving emotional awareness and regulation.

However, the ethical considerations surrounding the use of AI in emotional intelligence must be carefully navigated. Issues such as data privacy, algorithmic bias, and the potential for AI to perpetuate existing inequalities require thoughtful consideration and regulation. Additionally, reliance on AI-driven emotional intelligence tools should not replace human-to-human interactions or undermine the importance of empathy and genuine connection in fostering emotional intelligence.

Intersectionality and EI underscore the importance of recognizing and addressing the unique challenges faced by individuals with multiple marginalized identities, while the role of technology in shaping EI highlights both opportunities and ethical considerations in the digital age. By acknowledging and navigating these complexities, individuals and organizations can foster a more inclusive and technologically adept approach to EI development.

TAKEAWAYS

◆ **Emotional Intelligence (EI):** EI is a crucial skill in the modern business world, enabling individuals to understand and manage their emotions. It is particularly important in diverse workplaces that require adaptability, flexibility, and strong interpersonal skills.

◆ **EI for Women:** In male-dominated sectors, EI is more than just a professional asset. It is a transformative tool that allows women to navigate complex workplace dynamics, break down gender-based barriers, and create a more equitable environment. EI can lead to leadership roles, promote collaboration, and challenge traditional hierarchies, contributing to a more balanced representation of women in various industries.

◆ **Components of EI**: EI consists of four key components—self-awareness, self-regulation, empathy, and social skills. Each component is critical in managing emotions and engaging meaningfully with others.

◆ **Intersectionality and EI**: Intersectionality highlights how various aspects of identity intersect and shape individuals' experiences and opportunities. Recognizing and addressing the unique challenges faced by individuals with multiple marginalized identities is essential in the context of EI.

◆ **Strategies for Enhancing EI**: Cultivating EI habits involves integrating EI principles into daily life, creating a supportive environment, and engaging in regular feedback and reflection.

◆ **Technology and EI**: Technology, including digital communication platforms and AI-driven emotional intelligence tools, plays a significant role in shaping EI. However, it also presents ethical considerations that must be carefully navigated.

REFLECTIONS

☐ **Applying EI:**
  ▶ How can you apply the principles of EI in your daily interactions at work?
  ▶ Consider specific situations where EI could be beneficial and how to implement EI strategies in those scenarios.

☐ **Enhancing Self-Awareness and Self-Regulation:**
  ▶ What strategies can you employ to enhance your self-awareness and self-regulation?
  ▶ Consider techniques such as mindfulness, meditation, and deep breathing exercises and how to incorporate these techniques into your daily routine.

☐ **Intersectionality and EI:**
  ▶ How does your understanding of intersectionality influence your approach to EI?
  ▶ Reflect on your own identities and how they intersect and consider how this might impact your experience and practice of EI.

☐ **Technology and EI:**

  ▶ How can technology aid your EI development, and what are the ethical considerations?

  ▶ Consider the role of digital communication platforms and AI-driven emotional intelligence tools in shaping EI and reflect on the potential benefits and challenges these technologies present.

☐ **Creating a Supportive Environment:**

  ▶ How can you create a supportive environment in your workplace to foster the development of EI habits?

  ▶ Consider strategies for promoting open communication and emotional development, such as advocating for regular feedback sessions, engaging in team-building activities, or fostering an inclusive atmosphere.

☐ **EI for Women in Male-Dominated Industries:**

  ▶ How can you leverage EI as a woman in a male-dominated industry to navigate complex workplace dynamics and foster a more equitable environment?

  ▶ Reflect on specific challenges you might face in your industry and consider how EI could help you overcome these obstacles.

CHAPTER 10

Prioritizing Physical and Mental Well-Being

◆◆◆◆◆◆◆◆◆◆◆◆◆

As leaders, the daily grind often demands every ounce of our focus and energy, making it easy to overlook our health and well-being. The relentless pace of work, coupled with societal expectations that equate busyness with productivity and success, can create a toxic cycle that wears us down. I have experienced the negative impact of this mindset firsthand, seeing how the glorification of constant activity can lead to an unhealthy imbalance. For example, during the launch of a new project, I was working around the clock to meet tight deadlines. I often skipped meals, relied on coffee, and got only a few hours of sleep each night. This unsustainable routine eventually led to severe burnout, impacting both my physical health and my ability to effectively manage the business.

This prevailing attitude encourages us to prioritize work above all else, leading to harmful habits. In our drive to meet deadlines, we sacrifice sleep, neglect regular exercise, and opt for quick, unhealthy meals. The stress and pressure to constantly perform can erode our mental health, leading to a sense of disconnection from what truly matters. Despite these risks, the "hustle culture" continues to be celebrated, often at the expense of personal well-being.

In this whirlwind of constant activity, it is easy to forget that our health is a finite resource, one that requires care and attention. The warning by Jim Rohn, "Take care of your body, it is the only place you have to live," resonates deeply. It serves as a reminder that the success we pursue is meaningless without a healthy body and mind to enjoy it. To truly thrive, we need to shift our perspective, recognizing that our physical, mental, and spiritual health are fundamental to our success and happiness.

Achieving this balance requires intentionality. I found that prioritizing my life in a specific order—spirituality, my relationship with my husband, family, and then my career—has given me a sense of equilibrium. This approach allows me to navigate the demands of leadership while still honoring my health and relationships. It isn't always easy, but by taking small steps toward a more balanced lifestyle, I have seen significant improvements in my energy levels, mood, and overall satisfaction with life.

The journey toward balance is a personal one, and there's no one-size-fits-all solution. However, it is crucial for business leaders to make conscious choices that support their health and well-being. This might mean setting boundaries, dedicating time for exercise and meditation, or prioritizing quality time with loved ones. By doing so, we create a foundation that supports our careers and sustains us for the long haul. Ultimately, a business cannot thrive without a healthy and balanced leader at its helm. Consider the following strategies to create balance and ensure that you prioritize your physical and mental health.

Defining Work and Personal Life: The Importance of Boundaries

Setting boundaries between work and personal life is critical for maintaining a healthy work-life balance. When work encroaches on personal time, it can lead to stress, burnout, and strained relationships. To avoid these negative outcomes, establish clear limits on when work begins and ends. This involves designating specific work hours and committing to respecting those boundaries. By doing so, you create a structure that separates your professional responsibilities from your personal life, allowing you to recharge and focus on other important aspects of your life.

In my own experience, one of the most effective ways to set boundaries is by adhering to a consistent daily schedule. I make it a point to set my work hours and stick to them as much as possible. When I work from home, I create a designated workspace to help maintain the distinction between work and home life. The act of leaving that space at the end of the workday serves as a physical reminder that work is done, and it's time to transition to personal activities. This routine has been instrumental in helping me mentally switch gears, reducing stress and improving my focus when I am at work.

If you are in a relationship, it is also crucial to set aside dedicated time for your relationship. Evenings and weekends should be sanctuaries for relaxation, family, and hobbies. By safeguarding these times, you ensure that you are giving yourself a chance to rest and enjoy life outside of work. I've found it beneficial to set clear expectations with my colleagues and clients about my availability outside of work hours. They know that I will not respond to emails or phone calls after a certain time or during weekends unless it is an emergency. This clear communication has been effective in managing expectations and respecting boundaries.

Establishing and maintaining boundaries requires discipline, especially in a world where technology makes it easy to stay connected to work 24/7. However, the benefits of setting boundaries are significant. By creating a clear separation between work and personal life, you reduce stress, improve your overall well-being, and have more time for the people and activities you care about. This balance ultimately leads to greater productivity and satisfaction in both your career and personal life.

Learning to Say "No"

One of the most empowering skills you can cultivate is learning to say "no". It is a simple word, but it carries immense power. It is about understanding your limits. In our professional lives, we often find ourselves inundated with tasks and responsibilities. While it is important to be proactive and take on challenges, it is equally crucial to recognize when our plate is full. Saying "no" in such situations is not a sign of weakness or incompetence; rather, it is an assertion of self-awareness and respect for our own capacity.

When we say "no" to a task that we cannot accommodate, we say "yes" to maintaining our work-life balance, reducing stress, and preventing burnout. It allows us to focus on the tasks at hand and ensures we are not spreading ourselves too thin.

However, saying "no" requires tact. It requires being assertive, not aggressive. Explain your reasons clearly and offer alternatives if possible. Remember that saying "no" is not about rejecting the person but declining the task.

In my own experience, learning to say "no" has been a game-changer. It has helped me prioritize my well-being and become a more effective leader. It is a skill that takes practice, but the benefits are well worth the effort. For example, a client once requested an urgent project turnaround that would have required my team to work overtime for several weeks. Anticipating the potential for burnout and its impact on productivity, I respectfully declined. I explained that while we valued their business, taking on the project under such tight constraints would compromise both the quality of our work and my team's well-being. Instead, I proposed a more realistic timeline that ensured high-quality results without overburdening the team. The client appreciated the honesty and agreed to the revised schedule. This decision not only protected my team's health but also reinforced our commitment to delivering excellence.

Learning to say "no" is about setting boundaries and making mindful choices that support long-term success and well-being. By doing so, you create a sustainable work environment where you can thrive both personally and professionally.

Recharge and Refresh: Why Breaks Matter

Taking breaks throughout the day is a critical component of maintaining productivity, energy, and focus. Continuous work without rest can lead to fatigue, reduced efficiency, and, ultimately, burnout. By incorporating regular breaks into your routine, you give your mind and body a chance to recharge, which can improve your overall performance.

One effective technique for managing breaks is the Pomodoro Technique. This method involves working in focused intervals, typically 25 minutes, followed by a short break of about 5 minutes. After completing four intervals, you take a longer break of 15 to 30 minutes. This structured approach helps maintain concentration during work periods and provides a necessary mental reset during breaks. By breaking work into manageable segments, you avoid the feeling of overwhelm that can come from facing large tasks all at once.

In my experience, regular breaks provide a wellspring of creativity and problem-solving energy. When I step away from my work, even for a few minutes, I have found that it allows my brain to process information and form new connections. Some of my best ideas have come during these moments of respite. For example, while working on a complex project proposal, I took a short break to walk outside and clear my mind. During that walk, I had a breakthrough idea that significantly improved the proposal's structure and content. Furthermore, these breaks provide an opportunity to stretch, hydrate, or engage in light physical activity. This not only benefits my physical health but also helps reduce stress, making me more effective when I return to work.

Incorporating breaks into your day can also enhance your overall well-being. Taking time to step outside, breathe fresh air, or engage in a quick mindfulness exercise can reduce stress and boost your mood. By making breaks a regular part of your routine, you create a healthier and more sustainable work environment, leading to improved productivity and greater job satisfaction.

The Importance of Sleep: Building a Restful Routine

Sleep is essential for maintaining both physical and mental health, playing a crucial role in memory consolidation, mood regulation, and overall well-being. Prioritizing sleep means recognizing its importance and making intentional choices to ensure you get enough rest. To achieve this, it helps to create a consistent sleep schedule, aiming for at least seven hours of sleep each night. Consistency in your sleep-wake cycle helps regulate your body's internal clock, making it easier to fall asleep and wake up at the same time each day.

A key component of prioritizing sleep is developing a calming bedtime routine. This routine can include various activities that signal your body it is time to wind down. For example, reading a book, practicing meditation, or engaging in deep breathing exercises can help reduce stress and prepare your mind for sleep. The goal is to create a relaxing environment that promotes restful sleep, free from distractions or stimulating activities.

In my quest for a good night's sleep, I have found that creating an optimal sleep environment is paramount. For me, this means sparing no expense on a great mattress that provides the right balance of comfort and support. I have also invested in great pillows that cradle my head just right and soft bedding that feels like a gentle embrace. Maintaining a comfortable temperature, minimizing noise and light, and reducing screen time before bed are all crucial elements in setting the stage for restful sleep. You might also consider using blackout curtains, earplugs, or white noise machines to create a more peaceful sleep environment.

Prioritizing sleep can have a profound impact on your daily life. When you consistently get enough rest, you may notice improved focus, better decision-making, and enhanced mood. Quality sleep can also boost your immune system and reduce the risk of chronic health issues. By prioritizing sleep, you set the foundation for a healthier, more productive, and more fulfilling life.

Stay Active: The Benefits of Regular Exercise

Regular physical activity offers numerous benefits for both body and mind. Exercise can reduce stress, improve mood, boost energy levels, and even enhance sleep quality. Whether you prefer a morning run, pilates, or a workout at the gym, the key is to find activities that you enjoy and that fit into your lifestyle. Consistency is crucial, so aim for at least 30 minutes of moderate exercise most days of the week.

Even small amounts of activity throughout the day can make a difference. Simple activities like walking, stretching, or taking the stairs instead of the elevator contribute to a more active lifestyle. These minor changes can increase your energy and help you feel more alert and focused. Additionally, exercise can serve as a form of stress relief, providing a healthy outlet for releasing tension and clearing your mind.

To maintain motivation, consider setting fitness goals or joining a class or group activity. This not only keeps you accountable but also adds a social element to your exercise routine. By making regular exercise a part of your life, you can improve your overall well-being and build a stronger, more resilient body.

Admittedly, this is a struggle for me. Despite understanding the numerous benefits of regular physical activity, I find it challenging to maintain consistency in my exercise routine. The only time I am truly successful in this area is when I have a personal trainer holding me accountable, partly because I do not want to lose the money I have invested in a trainer. I am actively working on improving my consistency and making regular exercise a part of my life. It's a journey, and I am committed to making progress, one step at a time.

Fuel Your Body: The Importance of Healthy Eating

Good nutrition plays a crucial role in maintaining overall health and well-being. To eat healthily, focus on balanced meals that include a variety of fruits, vegetables, whole grains, and lean proteins. This approach provides your body with the essential nutrients it needs to function optimally and can help you maintain a healthy weight.

In my journey towards maintaining a healthy lifestyle, I found that preparation is key. I make it a point to keep healthy snacks at work, in my car, and even in my purse. This way, no matter where I am or how busy my schedule gets, I always have a nutritious option at hand. This small but significant habit has helped me resist the temptation of fast food and processed snacks and stay committed to my health goals. It is a practical strategy that I have incorporated into my lifestyle and has made a noticeable difference in my overall well-being.

Hydration is also vital. Aim to drink plenty of water throughout the day and limit sugary drinks and caffeine. By making conscious choices about what you eat and drink, you can support your physical health and improve your energy levels. Healthy eating can also boost your mood and contribute to a more positive outlook on life.

Cultivate Calm: The Power of Mindfulness

Mindfulness practices, such as meditation or deep breathing, offer powerful tools for managing stress and improving focus. By dedicating daily time to mindfulness, you can reduce anxiety and maintain a more balanced perspective. These practices encourage you to live in the present moment, allowing you to fully appreciate life and handle challenges with greater calmness.

Meditation is a popular form of mindfulness that can be done anywhere, whether at home, in the office, or outdoors. It involves focusing your attention on your breath, helping to quiet the mind and reduce stress. Deep breathing exercises, like box breathing or diaphragmatic breathing, are quick and effective techniques for calming the body and mind.

Guided relaxation sessions can also be beneficial, providing a structured approach to mindfulness. You can use apps or online resources to access a variety of guided sessions tailored to different needs and preferences. Incorporating mindfulness into your daily routine can lead to improved focus, enhanced creativity, and a greater sense of inner peace.

Strengthen Connections:
The Value of Social Relationships

Building and maintaining strong relationships with family, friends, and colleagues is vital for emotional well-being. These connections offer support, reduce stress, and foster a sense of community. Scheduling regular social activities, even virtual ones, can help you stay connected and maintain meaningful relationships.

Spending quality time with loved ones can provide joy and comfort. Whether it is a family dinner, a phone call with a friend, or a casual outing with colleagues, these moments provide opportunities to share experiences and create lasting memories. Social connections also serve as a buffer against stress, offering a supportive network to lean on during challenging times.

I have found that one of the most effective ways to maintain strong relationships is through shared meals. Rod and I have a cherished tradition of having dinner together every night when we are at home. We sit at the kitchen table and use this time to talk and connect. This tradition, which began in my childhood at my parents' home, has been a constant thread throughout my life. I carried it into my marriage, upheld it while raising our children, and continue to honor it today as empty nesters. This simple act is our glue, holding us together through the ebbs and flows of life.

It is also important to cultivate a sense of community within your workplace. Building strong relationships with colleagues can lead to a more positive work environment and improve teamwork. Simple gestures, like sharing a cup of coffee or offering a kind word, can strengthen these bonds and contribute to a more cohesive team.

I know the value of such relationships firsthand. During my tenure in the auto industry, I had the privilege of working with Yolanda Avalos. She was more than just a colleague; she was a confidante and accountability partner. Our relationship played a pivotal role in shaping me as a leader. Yolanda's insights and perspectives challenged me to think differently and approach problems from new angles. Her unwavering support and honest feedback helped me navigate complex projects and difficult decisions. While I didn't always like what she had to say, I knew her words came from a place of authenticity and genuine concern. Our friendship played a significant role in my professional growth, providing a foundation of trust and mutual respect that strengthened my leadership skills and confidence.

Seek Support: When to Ask for Professional Help

Despite your best efforts to manage stress and maintain balance, there may be times when you need additional support. This is not a reflection of failure, but rather an acknowledgment of our shared human condition. We all experience periods of struggle, and it is during these times that seeking professional help becomes a courageous and important step. Therapists and counselors are trained to offer guidance and coping strategies to help you navigate difficult emotions and life challenges. They provide an empathetic ear, a fresh perspective, and evidence-based strategies to help you manage your mental health.

Therapy can provide a safe space to discuss your feelings and work through personal issues. It is a place where you can be your authentic self without fear of judgment. Different types of therapy, such as cognitive-behavioral therapy (CBT) or mindfulness-based stress reduction (MBSR), offer effective techniques for managing stress and improving mental health. CBT, for instance, helps you understand how your thoughts, feelings, and behaviors interact, enabling you to break free from negative thought patterns. MBSR, on the other hand, teaches you to focus on the present moment, reducing stress and promoting relaxation.

Professional support can help you develop healthier thought patterns and coping mechanisms, leading to greater resilience and emotional well-being. With their guidance, you can learn to reframe negative thoughts, manage your emotions more effectively, and build a toolkit of strategies to handle future challenges. This process of personal growth can lead to a stronger sense of self, improved relationships, and a higher quality of life.

I had to learn that seeking help is not a sign of weakness but rather a sign of self-awareness and a commitment to my own well-being. For example, during a particularly stressful time when I was managing multiple projects alongside personal commitments, I began to feel overwhelmed and unable to cope. Realizing I needed support, I reached out to a therapist. Through our sessions, I gained valuable insights into my stress triggers and learned effective coping strategies. Taking this proactive step demonstrated strength, resilience, and a commitment to continuously improving my life.

You do not have to face challenges alone—professional help is available to guide you on your journey. Whether you're dealing with a temporary setback or a long-term issue, therapists and counselors can provide the support you need. They can help you navigate your path to recovery, empowering you to become the best version of yourself. So, when the going gets tough, know that it is okay to reach out for help. You are not alone, and with the right support, you can overcome your challenges and thrive.

Explore Passions:
The Joy of Hobbies and Interests

Engaging in hobbies and interests is a wonderful way to unwind, recharge, and add a splash of color to the canvas of life. Whether it's getting your hands dirty in the garden, creating a masterpiece with a paintbrush, strumming a melody on a guitar, or whipping up a culinary delight, pursuing activities that bring you joy adds balance to your life. These hobbies provide a welcome respite from work demands and offer a creative outlet for self-expression, allowing you to explore different facets of your personality.

Hobbies promote relaxation and stress relief by allowing you to focus on something you enjoy. Time spent engaging in hobbies creates a bubble where daily pressures cease to exist. This immersion in a joyful activity can lead to an improved mood, a greater sense of satisfaction, and a rejuvenated spirit. Additionally, hobbies often create opportunities to connect with others with similar interests. This fosters social bonds, builds a supportive community, and adds a sense of belonging.

Travel is one of my favorite hobbies. The thrill of exploring new places, immersing myself in diverse cultures, and creating memories in different corners of the world brings me immense joy. Traveling broadens my perspective, enriches my experiences, and fuels my passion for life. For example, during a trip to Australia, we explored the vibrant city of Sydney, marveled at the iconic Sydney Opera House, and enjoyed a scenic drive along the Great Ocean Road. These experiences not only deepened my appreciation of Australian culture but also provided a much-needed break from my daily routine.

Make time for hobbies by dedicating time each week to pursue your passions. This can be a specific "me-time" slot in your schedule, a sacred time where you indulge in what you love. This can help you maintain a healthy work-life balance, keep stress at bay, and ensure that you are not just surviving, but thriving.

Engaging in activities you love is a gentle reminder that life is about more than work—it is about finding joy in the simple things, creating moments that bring happiness, and cherishing the journey. Make time to cultivate joy in your life, because at the end of the day these are the moments that make life truly worth living.

Recognize Your Worth

There was a time during my corporate journey when I felt like an outsider, struggling to find my place in a seemingly cold and unwelcoming work environment. It was difficult to maintain my sense of self amid a few colleagues who were dismissive, condescending, and at times, downright mean. For example, during a business trip with colleagues, one of them was searching for another colleague with genuine concern. I jokingly asked if he ever looked for me like that, admiring his thoughtfulness. He replied, "No, why would I look for you?" That comment deeply hurt my feelings and left me feeling even more isolated.

I would return home from business trips feeling defeated as if my efforts had been in vain. My mind would spiral with thoughts of failure and self-doubt, questioning whether I was truly cut out for my chosen career path. During those times, my husband became my anchor, always ready to listen and offer words of comfort. He was patient and empathetic, yet there were moments when he grew frustrated, pointing out that I was allowing my colleagues' negativity to impact my emotional well-being.

During these challenging experiences, Rod would say, "If you want a friend, get a dog." Initially, his words stung, but they eventually revealed a profound truth: not everyone will like you, and some people will actively try to bring you down. Their negativity often stems from their own insecurities, envy, or misery, which they project onto others. But it is not their actions that define you; it is your response that shapes your path. Realizing this, I learned to distance myself from those who did not have my best interests at heart.

In retrospect, I wish I had understood this earlier in my career. Perhaps I could have avoided years spent in undervalued jobs with toxic colleagues and instead chosen environments that celebrated my uniqueness and encouraged growth. If I could offer one piece of advice, it would be this: never allow anyone to make you feel inferior. Surround yourself with positive influences, and do not waste time seeking approval from others. The key to progress is embracing your individuality and nurturing the qualities that make you unique. Your distinctiveness will light the way to a successful and fulfilling career.

Stay Grounded and Grateful

As you reach the pinnacle of your career, it is easy to get swept up in the excitement of success. But amid the accolades and achievements, remember to stay grounded and grateful. This attitude of humility and gratitude will keep you connected to your roots and guide you in extending grace and assistance to others. Remember the struggles you faced, the people who supported you, and the lessons you learned along the way.

As you rise, make a promise to yourself to never forget those who are still climbing. Use your success as a platform to mentor and inspire others. Offer guidance and support to those who need it, sharing your experiences and wisdom to help them navigate their own challenges. By doing so, you can create a positive ripple effect that extends far beyond your own journey.

The true measure of greatness is not just in achieving your own goals but in helping others achieve theirs. When you leverage your talents and resources to benefit others, you create a lasting legacy. Reinvest in your community, support those around you, and work towards a world where success is shared and celebrated by all. Together, we can build a brighter future, one where success is not a finite resource but a boundless opportunity for everyone.

So, as you celebrate your success, remember to stay humble, share your blessings, and continue to make a difference. Your impact will be felt not only in the accomplishments you achieve but in the lives you touch along the way. This is the true essence of success—a journey where we rise by lifting others.

TAKEAWAYS

◆ **Health is Wealth:** Prioritize your health and well-being over work. Your success is meaningless without a healthy body and mind.

◆ **Work-Life Balance:** Set clear boundaries between work and personal life. This balance is crucial for maintaining your overall well-being and preventing burnout.

◆ **Take Breaks:** Regular breaks are essential for maintaining productivity and focus. They give your mind and body a chance to recharge and can improve your overall performance.

◆ **Say "No":** By saying "no" to overcommitment, we say "yes" to balance, stress reduction, and prevention of burnout. This skill requires practice and tact, but its benefits are significant, leading to improved well-being and effective leadership.

◆ **Sleep is Essential:** Prioritize sleep and develop a consistent sleep schedule. Good sleep is crucial for maintaining both physical and mental health.

◆ **Stay Active:** Regular physical activity can reduce stress, improve mood, and boost energy levels. Find activities you enjoy and make them a part of your daily routine.

◆ **Eat Healthy:** Good nutrition is crucial for maintaining overall health and well-being. Make conscious choices about what you eat and drink.

◆ **Practice Mindfulness:** Incorporate mindfulness practices into your daily routine. These practices can help manage stress and improve focus.

◆ **Value Relationships:** Build and maintain strong relationships with family, friends, and colleagues. These connections offer emotional support and foster a sense of community.

◆ **Seek Help When Needed:** Don't hesitate to seek professional help if you are struggling with stress, anxiety, or other mental health issues.

◆ **Pursue Hobbies:** Engage in hobbies and interests to unwind and recharge. These activities can provide a break from work and offer a creative outlet for self-expression.

◆ **Recognize Your Worth:** Never allow anyone to make you feel inferior. Embrace your individuality and nurture the qualities that make you unique.

◆ **Stay Grounded:** Amid the excitement of success, remember to stay grounded and grateful.

REFLECTIONS

☐ **Prioritizing Physical and Mental Well-Being:**

  ▶ How can you better prioritize your health in your daily routine?

  ▶ What boundaries can you set to separate your work and personal life?

  ▶ Reflect on a recent situation where you felt overwhelmed with tasks. How could saying "no" help maintain your work-life balance and reduce stress?

  ▶ What steps can you take to be more comfortable saying "no" in the future?

  ▶ How can you incorporate regular breaks into your work routine?

  ▶ What steps can you take to improve your sleep habits?

  ▶ How can you incorporate regular physical activity into your daily routine?

  ▶ What changes can you make to your diet to improve your physical health and energy levels?

  ▶ How can you incorporate mindfulness practices into your daily routine?

  ▶ How can you strengthen your connections with family, friends, and colleagues?

  ▶ Are there any stressors or mental health issues that you need professional help to manage?

  ▶ What hobbies or interests can you explore to add balance to your life?

  ▶ How can you better recognize and celebrate your worth?

  ▶ How can you stay grounded and grateful amid success?

◆◆◆◆◆◆◆◆◆◆◆◆◆◆◆◆◆◆◆◆

PART III

Thriving as a Leader and Communicator

The essence of leadership lies in fostering growth, mastering the language of impact, and navigating toward a sustainable future with a vision that unites and inspires. – Tammie Ross

CHAPTER 11

From Glass Ceilings to Growth – Celebrating Female Leadership

◆◆◆◆◆◆◆◆◆◆◆◆◆

Traditional leadership paradigms, characterized by assertiveness and hierarchical structures, can marginalize women and their unique strengths in leadership roles. These models often prioritize traits typically associated with masculinity, such as dominance and decisiveness, while undervaluing qualities like empathy and collaboration.

As Nick Hernandez, CEO of 360 Learning, points out, a top-down approach to management can stifle decision-making skills and turn individuals into mere executors of instructions rather than empowering them to become leaders. This approach is not only detrimental to employees but also to managers, who are burdened with the pressure of providing answers and advice on every topic. Hernandez advocates for a leadership style that promotes autonomy and trusts teams to manage independently, underscoring the importance of empowering employees to cultivate their leadership skills.[1]

Hierarchical structures within organizations can create significant barriers to female advancement, reinforcing traditional power dynamics that favor men. Women often face challenges asserting their leadership in environments that prioritize top-down decision-making and rigid hierarchies. Traditional leadership models also tend to overlook the importance of emotional intelligence and relationship-building, which are areas where women often excel.

By emphasizing assertiveness over empathy, traditional models may fail to harness the full potential of diverse leadership styles, limiting innovation and stifling organizational growth. Therefore, adopting more inclusive and collaborative approaches that empower individuals to make decisions and develop leadership skills is essential for creating environments where women can thrive and contribute their unique perspectives to drive organizational success.

Persistent Challenges for Women in Leadership

Despite progress toward gender equality, pervasive biases, and invisible barriers continue to obstruct the advancement of women into leadership roles. The concept of the glass ceiling, which limits upward mobility for women within organizations, remains a significant obstacle. Women often encounter implicit biases that undermine their credibility and competence, leading to missed career opportunities. Additionally, workplace cultures that prioritize long hours and a "work hard, play hard" mentality can disadvantage women who require flexibility to balance professional and personal responsibilities. These norms perpetuate gender stereotypes and reinforce the belief that leadership is inherently masculine, further sidelining female leaders.

Furthermore, women of color and those from marginalized communities face intersectional barriers that significantly compound the challenges they experience in advancing their careers. The intersection of gender and race can intensify biases and discrimination, presenting additional hurdles for women striving to shatter the glass ceiling. Despite aspirations for higher-level roles and the potential to excel, women continue to navigate systemic barriers and outdated norms that impede their professional growth.

Marsha Guerrier, founder of HerSuiteSpot, a network supporting women as leaders and entrepreneurs, highlights the importance of professional development and recognition in career advancement. However, women, particularly women of color, often lack access to these opportunities in the workplace, leading to feelings of invisibility and discouragement. Moreover, female managers are less likely than their male counterparts to feel included in key networks within their organizations, further exacerbating their challenges in reaching senior leadership positions. As Kimberly Lee Minor, founder of Women of Color in Retail, notes, "historical societal biases and outdated norms continue to hinder progress, perpetuating gender disparities in leadership."[2]

Unlocking Innovation Through Diverse Leadership Perspectives

Diverse leadership perspectives are instrumental in driving innovation and fostering inclusive organizational cultures. Research by Sylvia Ann Hewlett, based on a comprehensive survey of 1,800 professionals, 40 case studies, and numerous focus groups and interviews, provides strong evidence that companies with diverse leadership excel in innovation and market growth. Hewlett's research identified that companies with two-dimensional (2D) diversity—where leaders have at least three inherent diversity traits (such as gender, race, or age) and three acquired diversity traits (like global experience, language skills, or cultural knowledge)—significantly outperform those without this diversity. Employees at these companies are 45% more likely to report increased market share and 70% more likely to report capturing a new market segment, demonstrating the tangible benefits of embracing a variety of leadership styles and backgrounds.[3]

The reason diverse leadership is so effective lies in the unique perspectives and experiences each leader brings to the table. When leaders come from varied backgrounds, they approach problems with different viewpoints, leading to more comprehensive and creative solutions. This variety of experiences enriches decision-making processes, allowing organizations to better navigate complex challenges. For example, women in leadership often bring compassion, intuition, and consensus-building skills, which can enhance team dynamics and promote cross-collaboration. This inclusive approach encourages open communication and a collaborative work environment, fostering a culture of innovation.

However, despite the clear benefits, a significant portion of companies still lack 2-D diversity in leadership. Hewlett's research revealed that 78% of respondents work at companies without diverse leadership, indicating that many organizations miss out on the advantages diversity offers. This lack of diversity has broader implications beyond internal culture—it can impact a company's ability to reach and understand diverse markets. When leadership lacks diversity, innovative ideas from women, people of color, and LGBT individuals are less likely to be endorsed. Women are 20% less likely than heterosexual white men to have their ideas accepted, people of color are 24% less likely, and LGBT individuals are 21% less likely.[4] This disparity can lead to a significant loss of market opportunities, as these underrepresented groups often have insights into unmet needs in under-leveraged markets.

Moreover, when leadership reflects a narrow demographic, companies risk alienating a significant portion of their workforce and customer base. A diverse leadership team can better understand the needs and perspectives of a diverse employee base and clientele, creating an environment where everyone feels valued, seen, and heard. This inclusivity can drive employee engagement and retention, as team members are more likely to stay with a company where they feel represented and understood.

Embracing diverse leadership perspectives is not just about creating an inclusive work-place; it is a strategic imperative for fostering innovation and achieving market growth. Companies with 2D diversity are better positioned to navigate complex challenges, capture new markets, and build a cohesive organizational culture. By prioritizing diversity in leadership, organizations can unlock the full potential of their teams, fostering creativity, innovation, and sustained success.

Key Competencies for Effective Leadership

Leadership excellence relies on a combination of skills and behaviors that enable leaders to guide their teams toward success. Among the most critical competencies is the ability to adopt a results-oriented approach. Effective leaders set clear objectives, creating a sense of direction and purpose for their teams. This approach involves outlining SMART goals that drive performance and help team members understand what is expected of them. Leaders who prioritize results instill a culture of accountability, where each team member is responsible for their role in achieving collective outcomes.

In addition to focusing on results, effective leaders possess strong strategic thinking skills. They can navigate complex challenges, analyze various scenarios, and make informed decisions that align with long-term goals. Strategic leaders are adept at forecasting potential obstacles and opportunities, allowing them to plan and allocate resources efficiently. This foresight is crucial for sustaining organizational success and fostering resilience in the face of uncertainty. Strategic leaders can also balance short-term priorities with long-term objectives, ensuring that the team remains on track while adapting to changing circumstances.

Effective communication is another essential competency for successful leaders. They can clearly articulate their vision, values, and expectations to their teams, creating a shared sense of purpose. Communication is not just about speaking; it involves active listening and being receptive to feedback. Leaders who communicate effectively build strong relationships with their teams, fostering trust and collaboration. By leading by example, these leaders set the tone for the organization's culture, demonstrating the behaviors and values they expect from others. This approach inspires others to take ownership of their roles and contributes to a positive and productive work environment.

Personal and professional development are also central to leadership excellence. True achievers continually seek growth opportunities, viewing challenges as a means of self-improvement. By adopting a growth mindset, leaders encourage a culture of learning and development within their teams. This mindset emphasizes that abilities can be developed through dedication and hard work, fostering innovation and creativity. Leaders who embrace this mindset inspire their teams to take risks, explore new ideas, and pursue continuous improvement.

Each of these competencies—results orientation, strategic thinking, effective communication, and a growth mindset—plays a pivotal role in a leader's capacity to drive change and create a lasting impact. By embodying these traits, leaders can build high-performing teams, navigate challenges confidently, and foster a culture of excellence. Ultimately, these competencies not only contribute to organizational success but also help leaders leave a positive and enduring legacy.

The Power of Listening in Leadership

Corine Jansen's research on listening suggests that women process emotional components of communication more effectively than men, utilizing both hemispheres of the brain more symmetrically for processing messages, while men typically rely more on the left hemisphere. This distinction may lead to the misconception that listening is less action-oriented or indicative of weakness.[5]

However, listening, especially empathetic listening, is crucial in leadership. Women are often recognized for their proficiency in empathetic listening, which involves understanding not just spoken words but also the underlying emotions and intentions. This skill fosters trust and understanding, creating a supportive and inclusive workplace.

Jessica Rivera, a strategic business coach and founder of JR Coaching, underscores the transformative impact of effective communication in leadership. She emphasizes the importance of not only the content of leaders' communications but also their delivery, ensuring messages resonate and empower. Rivera's approach promotes the idea that impactful leadership is deeply rooted in authentic connections and empathy, where leaders actively listen to elevate those around them.[6]

Effective listeners can recognize diverse viewpoints and integrate them into the decision-making process. Women leaders who excel in listening foster open communication and collaboration, leading to innovative solutions and a unified team dynamic. Strong listening skills also play a critical role in conflict resolution, allowing leaders to understand all sides of an issue and facilitate constructive dialogues. This capability resolves disputes and prevents their escalation, promoting a harmonious work environment.

Empathy as a Catalyst for Female Leadership

Empathy—the capacity to understand and share the feelings of another—is a cornerstone of effective leadership, particularly in team-based settings. When leaders demonstrate empathy, they send a powerful message to their team: that each member is important, their opinions are valued, and their experiences are acknowledged. This fosters a sense of belonging, which is crucial for team cohesion and morale. When team members feel understood, they are more likely to engage fully in their work, contribute their best ideas, and collaborate effectively with others.

Empathy also plays a significant role in resolving conflicts and addressing workplace issues. By approaching problems with an empathetic mindset, leaders can understand the underlying emotions and motivations of their team members. This understanding allows them to address issues at their root, rather than just treating the symptoms. It also helps in finding solutions that consider the needs and concerns of all parties involved, leading to more harmonious outcomes.

In addition to conflict resolution, empathy is vital for motivating and inspiring teams. When leaders take the time to understand what drives their team members, they can tailor their approach to meet individual needs. This personalized approach creates a sense of appreciation and respect, fostering loyalty and commitment to the team's objectives. Empathetic leaders are more likely to inspire their teams to go the extra mile because they have established a strong emotional connection with them.

Moreover, empathy is a critical factor in building trust within the team. Trust is the glue that holds teams together, and it is built when leaders consistently demonstrate that they understand and care about their team members. Trust allows teams to work more cohesively, take risks, and innovate without fear of failure. It also encourages a sense of accountability, as team members feel a personal responsibility to support their colleagues and contribute to the team's success.

Empathy is not a one-time effort but an ongoing practice that requires consistent attention and development. Leaders who cultivate empathy in their interactions with their teams create a workplace environment that is conducive to growth, collaboration, and innovation. By walking in another's shoes, leaders can bridge gaps, build strong relationships, and foster a sense of unity and purpose within the team.

Empowering Women Leaders Through Data-Driven Strategies

Despite their capabilities, women in leadership roles are often not immediately recognized for their strategic and data-driven acumen. This oversight not only underestimates their potential but also overlooks a crucial aspect of modern leadership—proficiency in data utilization. Research from *Three Keys to Building a Data-Driven Strategy*, a McKinsey Digital article, shows that companies embracing data-driven strategies are substantially more likely to achieve competitive advantages, including a 23-fold increase in customer acquisition, a six-fold improvement in customer retention, and a 19-fold increase in profitability.[7]

Organizations can empower women leaders by implementing robust customer relationship management (CRM) systems to enhance customer relationship management and analytics, fostering a culture of data literacy with appropriate training, and regularly updating key performance indicators to reflect changing market conditions and company objectives. By adopting these strategies, organizations support women leaders in effectively using data-driven insights, maximizing their contributions, and dispelling biases regarding their strategic capabilities. Women, equipped with data-driven insights, can lead organizations to new heights of efficiency and profitability.

This chapter underscores the need to reevaluate and redefine traditional leadership models to better accommodate and harness the unique strengths that women bring to leadership roles. By breaking down the systemic barriers of the glass ceiling and challenging biases that restrict female advancement, we pave the way for more inclusive and equitable workplaces. Emphasizing the power of diverse leadership perspectives, we recognize the importance of fostering environments that value empathy, collaboration, and emotional intelligence.

By advocating for robust, data-driven strategies and cultivating key leadership competencies, we empower women leaders to excel and reshape their organizations. It is through these comprehensive and inclusive approaches that leadership can truly evolve to meet the demands of modern, diverse societies, making significant strides toward a balanced representation across all levels of management and leadership.

TAKEAWAYS

◆ **Redefining Leadership Paradigms:** Traditional leadership models often marginalize women's unique strengths in leadership roles. Adopting more inclusive and collaborative approaches that value empathy and collaboration can create environments where women can thrive and contribute their unique perspectives.

◆ **Persistent Challenges for Women in Leadership:** Despite progress toward gender equality, pervasive biases, and invisible barriers continue to obstruct the advancement of women into leadership roles. Women, particularly women of color, often face intersectional barriers that compound the challenges they experience in advancing their careers.

◆ **Unlocking Innovation Through Diverse Leadership Perspectives:** Diverse leadership perspectives are instrumental in driving innovation and fostering inclusive organizational cultures. Companies with diverse leadership excel in innovation and market growth.

◆ **Key Competencies for Effective Leadership:** Leadership excellence relies on a combination of skills and behaviors, including a results-oriented approach, strategic thinking, effective communication, and a growth mindset.

◆ **The Power of Listening in Leadership:** Effective listening, especially empathetic listening, is crucial in leadership. Women leaders who excel in listening foster open communication and collaboration, leading to innovative solutions and a unified team dynamic.

◆ **Empathy as a Catalyst for Female Leadership:** Empathy—the capacity to under-stand and share the feelings of another—is a cornerstone of effective leadership. Leaders who demonstrate empathy foster a sense of belonging, which is crucial for team cohesion and morale.

◆ **Empowering Women Leaders through Data-Driven Strategies:** Women in leadership roles are often not immediately recognized for their strategic and data-driven acumen. Organizations can empower women leaders by implementing robust CRM systems, fostering a culture of data literacy, and regularly updating key performance indicators.

◆ **Embracing Diverse Leadership Perspectives:** Advocating for robust, data-driven strategies can empower women leaders to excel and reshape their organizations. It also underscores the need to reevaluate and redefine traditional leadership models to better accommodate and harness the unique strengths that women bring to leadership roles.

REFLECTIONS

☐ **Redefining Leadership Paradigms:**
  ▶ How can organizations shift from traditional, hierarchical leadership models to more inclusive and collaborative approaches?
  ▶ What steps can be taken to value and leverage women's unique strengths in leadership roles?

☐ **Challenges for Women in Leadership:**
  ▶ What are some examples of systemic barriers and biases women face in their professional advancement?
  ▶ How can these challenges be addressed at both the individual and organi-zational levels?

☐ **The Power of Diverse Leadership:**
  ▶ How does diverse leadership drive innovation and foster inclusive organiza-tional cultures?
  ▶ Can you think of examples where diverse leadership perspectives have led to tangible benefits in your own professional experience?

☐ **Key Competencies for Effective Leadership:**

▶ How can leaders cultivate key competencies such as a results-oriented approach, strategic thinking, effective communication, and a growth mindset?

▶ What strategies can be used to develop these skills?

☐ **The Role of Empathy and Listening in Leadership:**

▶ How can leaders improve their listening skills and demonstrate empathy in team interactions?

▶ What impact can these skills have on team dynamics and organizational culture?

☐ **Empowering Women through Data-Driven Strategies:**

▶ How can organizations support women leaders in effectively using data-driven insights?

▶ What role does data literacy play in this process, and how can it be fostered within organizations?

CHAPTER 12

Mastering Communication Skills

◆◆◆◆◆◆◆◆◆◆◆◆◆◆

The ability to communicate effectively, both verbally and in writing, is a critical skill that every leader must master to thrive in the business world. Clear, confident communication fosters professional respect and cultivates robust relationships. As a leader, you share your ideas, thoughts, and opinions across various contexts: meetings, networking events, speaking engagements, or personal discussions with colleagues and subordinates. Your words wield immense power—they can either build or destroy your business.

Articulateness, logical reasoning, and thorough preparation are essential communication traits. These skills are particularly significant for women who often face additional barriers and stereotypes. Effective communication becomes a tool to challenge those stereotypes and inspire fresh perspectives. Strive to communicate concisely, striking the right balance between providing essential information (without over-explaining) and getting straight to the point is a skill that matures over time.

Peter Drucker, known as the inventor of modern management, once said, "The most important thing in communication is to hear what isn't being said." This succinctly captures another aspect of effective communication—non-verbal communication cues.

Pay attention to your posture, your ability to maintain eye contact, and the tone and inflection of your voice. These nonverbal skills can either exhibit confidence or dilute your message and lose your audience's interest.

Remember, communication extends beyond spoken words. Written communication—text messages, emails, or any other form of correspondence—holds equal weight. Each word you write acts as a spotlight on your character. Precision and care in your writing are key—choose your words wisely to convey your message and avoid confusion. Here are some additional steps to enhance your communication skills:

Practice and Prepare: Allocate sufficient time to practice speeches or presentations, refining your message for maximum clarity and impact. Preparation also reduces stress and improves confidence.

Seek Feedback: Constructive criticism from mentors, colleagues, or trusted friends can identify areas for improvement and refine your communication style. Embrace feedback as a path to growth.

Take a Business Writing Course: Consider enrolling in a business writing course to hone your written communication skills. These classes offer valuable techniques to craft compelling, professional content.

Pay Attention to Detail: Always use spell check and grammar tools to eliminate errors. Proofread thoroughly before sharing written work. These simple steps enhance your professionalism.

Read Extensively: Reading can broaden your vocabulary and improve communication skills. Exposure to diverse literature expands your knowledge and refines your writing.

Join Toastmasters International: This supportive community helps you improve your public speaking skills. Through Toastmasters, you can build confidence, refine your delivery, and connect with others on a journey of self-improvement.

Mastering communication, both verbal and written, is essential for effective leadership. By honing these skills, you pave the way for a more successful and meaningful career in business and beyond.

The Art of Effective Listening

Effective listening is more than a passive act of hearing; it's an active process that requires full engagement with the speaker. In her book, *The Art of Listening: How People Feel Heard, Valued, and Understood*, Heather R. Younger provides the following strategies to help hone listening skills:[1]

Active Listening: Involves fully engaging with the speaker to understand their message. Give the speaker your full attention, make eye contact, and use nonverbal cues like nodding to show you are engaged. This approach demonstrates respect and encourages the speaker to continue sharing their thoughts.

Avoid Interruptions: Interrupting disrupts the flow of conversation and can make the speaker feel undervalued. To be an effective listener, resist the urge to interject and allow the speaker to finish their thoughts. This shows respect and gives you time to process the information.

Reflect and Paraphrase: Reflecting and paraphrasing are techniques that confirm you have understood the speaker's message. After they have spoken, summarize what you have heard in your own words and ask for confirmation. This demonstrates your attentiveness and allows for any corrections if you have misunderstood something.

Ask Open-Ended Questions: To deepen the conversation and show genuine interest, ask open-ended questions, encouraging the speaker to elaborate. These questions often start with "how," "what," or "why." By encouraging the speaker to share more, you foster a more meaningful dialogue and gain deeper insights.

Show Empathy: Empathy involves understanding and sharing the feelings of others. When listening, try to put yourself in the speaker's shoes and consider their emotions. You can express empathy by acknowledging their feelings and responding with supportive language to build trust and strengthen the connection between you and the speaker.

Focus on the Speaker: Effective listening requires complete focus on the speaker. Avoid distractions, such as checking your phone or multitasking. By giving your full attention, you show that you value the speaker's words and perspective.

Practice Patience: Patience is key to effective listening. Allow the speaker time to express themselves without rushing them. If there is a pause, resist the urge to fill it with your own thoughts. This patience creates a comfortable environment for open communication.

Provide Feedback: After listening, offer constructive feedback or respond with your own thoughts, ensuring they align with what the speaker shared. This feedback can include your reaction to their message, your agreement or disagreement, and any additional insights. Providing feedback closes the loop and demonstrates that you are engaged in the conversation.

Mastering effective listening can significantly improve your communication skills, strengthen relationships, and foster collaboration. By applying these techniques, you will create a more positive and open environment for meaningful conversations, allowing you to connect with others on a deeper level.

Strategies for Difficult Conversations

Difficult conversations are an inevitable part of our personal and professional lives. Whether addressing underperforming employees, negotiating with clients, or discussing sensitive topics with loved ones, these interactions require finesse. The following strategies from *Difficult Conversations: How to Discuss What Matters Most*, can be employed when handling tough conversations:[2]

Decipher the Underlying Structure: Recognize that difficult conversations are rarely about factual accuracy. Instead, they involve conflicting perceptions, interpretations, and values. Focus on understanding the deeper dynamics at play rather than fixating on who is right or wrong.

Start Without Defensiveness: Initiate conversations with openness and curiosity. Avoid triggering defensive reactions by framing your approach positively.

Stay Balanced: Maintain emotional equilibrium even when faced with attacks or accusations. Arguing inhibits learning about the other person's perspective. Emotions can run high during challenging discussions, but it is essential to stay calm and composed. Take deep breaths, speak slowly, and maintain a steady tone. If emotions escalate, consider pausing the conversation to regain composure. Remaining calm demonstrates respect and encourages the other person to respond similarly.

Choose the Right Setting: The environment where the conversation takes place can significantly impact its outcome. Opt for a private and comfortable setting where interruptions are minimized. This creates a safe space for open and honest communication, allowing both parties to focus on the conversation without distractions.

Use Active Listening: Active listening is crucial during difficult conversations. Give the other person your full attention, maintain eye contact, and avoid interrupting. Reflect on their words by paraphrasing what you have heard, showing that you understand their perspective. This approach fosters empathy and builds trust, creating a more collaborative atmosphere.

Focus on the Issue, Not the Person: When addressing a difficult topic, concentrate on the issue at hand rather than attacking or criticizing the person. Use "I" statements to express your feelings and avoid blaming language. This approach helps reduce defensiveness and promotes a constructive dialogue, allowing both parties to work towards a solution.

Be Honest and Transparent: Honesty is key to effective communication. Clearly express your thoughts, feelings, and concerns, and avoid sugarcoating the message. While it is important to be direct, do so with compassion and understanding. Being transparent fosters trust and paves the way for open dialogue.

Offer Solutions and Compromises: A productive, difficult conversation should aim to find solutions or compromises. Encourage a collaborative approach by inviting the other person to share their ideas for resolving the issue. Brainstorming together can lead to creative solutions and strengthen the relationship by fostering teamwork and cooperation.

Follow Up and Reflect: After the conversation, follow up with the other party to ensure that any agreed upon actions are taken. This demonstrates your commitment to resolving the issue and maintaining a positive relationship. Reflect on the conversation to identify what went well and what could be improved for future discussions.

By applying these strategies, you can confidently navigate difficult conversations and create a more positive and constructive environment for addressing sensitive topics. While challenging, these conversations are opportunities for growth, understanding, and building stronger connections with others.

Understanding Nonverbal Communication

Nonverbal communication is the silent language that plays a significant role in how we communicate. It encompasses facial expressions, body language, gestures, eye contact, posture, and even the tone and pitch of our voice. Learning to interpret and use nonverbal cues effectively can greatly enhance your communication skills, allowing you to connect with others and convey messages without saying a word. In his book, *Understanding Nonverbal Communication: A Semiotic Guide*, Marcel Danesi provides the following practical advice for developing awareness of nonverbal communication cues:[3]

The Power of Body Language: Body language refers to the physical movements and gestures that accompany verbal communication. It can reveal emotions, indicate agreement or disagreement, and express interest or disinterest. To make a positive impression, maintain an open and relaxed posture. Avoid crossing your arms, which might signal defensiveness, and instead, use open gestures to convey approachability.

Facial Expressions: Your face can express a wide range of emotions, from happiness and surprise to anger and sadness. When engaging in conversation, be aware of your facial expressions and ensure they align with your words. A genuine smile can instantly create a welcoming atmosphere, while raised eyebrows or furrowed brows can indicate curiosity or concern.

Eye Contact: Eye contact is a crucial aspect of nonverbal communication. It shows attentiveness and interest in the conversation. However, maintaining eye contact for too long can feel intimidating, while avoiding it can suggest dishonesty or disinterest. Aim for a balanced approach, where you maintain eye contact but also look away occasionally to create a comfortable interaction.

Gestures: Gestures add emphasis and clarity to your communication. They can include hand movements, head nods, or other physical cues that complement your words. When using gestures, ensure they are appropriate and not excessive, as too many can be distracting. Simple gestures, like nodding in agreement or using hand motions to highlight key points, can enhance your message.

Posture and Movement: Your posture and movement can reveal a lot about your attitude and confidence. Standing or sitting up straight with your shoulders back conveys confidence, while slouching can suggest disinterest or lack of energy. Pay attention to your movements as well. Pacing back and forth or fidgeting can indicate nervousness, while standing still and maintaining steady movements can project confidence and stability.

Tone and Pitch: Nonverbal communication also includes the tone and pitch of your voice. A calm, steady tone can create a sense of reassurance, while a high-pitched or loud voice might signal anxiety or aggression. Varying your tone and pitch can add emphasis and keep the conversation engaging.

Personal Space: Personal space, or proxemics, refers to the distance between you and others during communication. Different cultures have varying norms for personal space, so it is important to be aware of these differences. In general, maintain an appropriate distance to respect others' comfort zones. Standing too close can be intrusive, while standing too far away can seem disengaged.

Understanding nonverbal communication is key to effective interactions. By being mindful of your body language, facial expressions, eye contact, gestures, posture, and other nonverbal cues, you can convey confidence, build rapport, and communicate more effectively with others. Mastering these skills will help you easily navigate social situations and strengthen your ability to meaningfully connect with others.

Cultural Communication

Cultural communication refers to how people from diverse cultural backgrounds interact, share information, and understand each other. It involves recognizing and respecting cultural differences, adapting communication styles, and fostering an inclusive environment. This section explores the significance of cultural communication and why it is essential for successful project outcomes. Consider the following strategies to foster a culturally sensitive work environment:

Embrace Diversity: The construction industry often involves a mix of professionals from various cultural backgrounds, including architects, engineers, contractors, laborers, and clients. Embracing diversity means acknowledging and valuing these differences. By fostering an inclusive environment, teams can harness the unique perspectives and skills of each member, leading to more innovative solutions and a richer work environment.

Enhance Collaboration: Effective cultural communication enhances collaboration by promoting understanding among team members. When people feel their cultural backgrounds are respected, they are likelier to contribute ideas and work together harmoniously. This collaborative atmosphere reduces misunderstandings and promotes a sense of unity, which is essential in the fast-paced construction industry.

Avoid Misinterpretations: Cultural differences can lead to misinterpretations if not professionally managed. For example, gestures, eye contact, and body language can vary significantly across cultures. A gesture that is considered friendly in one culture might be offensive in another. By understanding these nuances, professionals can avoid misunderstandings and ensure clear communication.

Adapt Communication Styles: Adapting communication styles to suit diverse audiences is key to effective cultural communication. This involves recognizing that different cultures have varying preferences for directness, hierarchy, formality, and conflict resolution. Adapting your style to suit the cultural context can improve efficiency and reduce friction.

Build Trust and Relationships: Cultural communication is vital in building trust and relationships. When people from different backgrounds work together, trust is essential for project success. By showing cultural sensitivity and respect, you can build stronger relationships with colleagues, clients, and stakeholders. This trust fosters open communication and facilitates smoother project coordination.

Ensure Safety and Compliance: In construction, safety and compliance with regulations are paramount. Effective cultural communication ensures that all team members understand safety protocols and guidelines, regardless of their cultural background. Miscommunication in this area can have profound consequences, making cultural competence a critical factor in maintaining a safe work environment.

Enhance Client Relations: Clients in the construction industry come from various cultures and may have different expectations regarding communication and project management. By understanding their cultural background and adapting your communication style, you can build stronger client relationships. This approach not only improves customer satisfaction but also increases the likelihood of repeat business and referrals.

Cultural communication is a vital skill. By embracing diversity, adapting communication styles, and building trust through cultural sensitivity, professionals can create a more harmonious and effective work environment. This approach not only leads to successful project outcomes but also fosters a more inclusive and respectful work environment.

Mastering Negotiations in Construction

Negotiation skills are essential in the construction industry, serving as a key factor in successful project outcomes. Studies suggest that women often hesitate to negotiate due to societal expectations and the fear of backlash. This reluctance can lead to missed opportunities, wage gaps, and limited career advancement. Acknowledging these disparities is the first step toward developing strategies to overcome them. Consider these strategies for navigating and excelling in negotiations.

Build Confidence: Women can address the confidence gap through regular self-reflection and professional development programs. These activities help women recognize their achievements and gain valuable tools and knowledge to build their confidence. By focusing on personal growth, women can thrive and excel in their careers.

Communicate Assertively: Effective communication is critical for negotiation success. Women negotiators should prioritize assertiveness while maintaining professionalism. This involves clearly articulating thoughts, avoiding qualifiers that might undermine their position, and mastering active listening to understand the other party's needs. By refining these skills, women can navigate complex negotiations and achieve favorable outcomes.

Challenge Stereotypes: Women can overcome stereotypes by emphasizing their expertise, highlighting their accomplishments, and presenting well-reasoned arguments. This approach not only benefits individual negotiators but also contributes to a more equitable environment for everyone.

Embrace Collaboration: Projects can involve various stakeholders, each with unique goals. Women negotiators can leverage collaborative strategies emphasizing shared objectives and promoting teamwork among all parties. This approach fosters open communication, leading to smoother negotiations.

Develop a Negotiation Toolkit: Utilizing data-driven tools, such as market research, analytics, and case studies, can significantly strengthen a negotiator's position. By building a well-prepared toolkit, women gain credibility and confidence to advocate for their interests.

Negotiate Fair Compensation: Advocating for fair compensation is not just a personal gain; it is a stride towards gender equality in the workforce. To negotiate effectively, it is crucial to be armed with comprehensive data and industry benchmarks. Platforms like Payscale.com, Salary.com, and cbiz.com offer compensation studies and extensive databases of salary information based on job title, industry, and region. These sites provide personalized salary reports, salary calculators, and comparison tools. This not only helps assert one's worth but also underscores the positive impact of pay equity on the company's success. By leveraging these resources, women can present a compelling case for fair pay, demonstrating their value and the benefits of pay equity to the company's success.

By utilizing these strategies, women can improve their negotiation skills and pave the way for a more diverse and inclusive industry. With each successful negotiation, they not only advance their careers but also contribute to breaking down barriers for future generations.

TAKEAWAYS

◆ **Mastering Communication Skills:** Effective communication is a cornerstone of business success. It involves being concise, clear, and coherent. Regular practice, seeking feedback, and continuous learning can enhance your communication skills.

◆ **The Art of Effective Listening**: Active listening is a fundamental communication skill. It involves fully engaging with the speaker, avoiding interruptions, reflecting and paraphrasing, and asking open-ended questions.

◆ **Strategies for Difficult Conversations**: Navigating difficult conversations effectively involves preparation, choosing the right setting, active listening, staying calm and composed, focusing on the issue, being honest and transparent, offering solutions and compromises, and following up and reflecting.

◆ **Understanding Nonverbal Communication**: Nonverbal communication plays a significant role in communicating. It includes body language, facial expressions, eye contact, gestures, posture, tone and voice pitch, and personal space.

◆ **Cultural Communication**: Cultural communication involves recognizing and respecting cultural differences, adapting communication styles, and fostering an inclusive environment. It is essential for successful project outcomes.

◆ **Mastering Negotiations in Construction**: Negotiation skills are essential in the construction industry. It involves understanding the negotiation process, preparing thoroughly, building relationships, communicating effectively, and seeking win-win outcomes.

REFLECTIONS

☐ **Mastering Communication Skills:**

 ▶ How can you apply the principles of conciseness, clarity, and coherence in your daily communication?

 ▶ Can you recall a situation where effective communication made a significant difference?

☐ **The Art of Effective Listening:**

 ▶ How often do you practice active listening?

 ▶ Can you identify a recent conversation where you could have applied these techniques for a better outcome?

☐ **Strategies for Difficult Conversations:**

▶ Reflect on a recent difficult conversation you had. How did you handle it? What could you have done differently?

☐ **Understanding Nonverbal Communication:**

▶ Are you aware of your nonverbal cues when communicating with others?

▶ Can you identify any habits that you need to change?

☐ **Cultural Communication:**

▶ How diverse is your current environment, and how do you navigate cultural differences?

▶ Can you recall a situation where cultural communication played a significant role?

☐ **Mastering Negotiations:**

▶ How comfortable are you with negotiation?

▶ What strategies do you use, and how can you improve them?

CHAPTER 13

Shaping a Sustainable Tomorrow with Community-Centric Leadership

◆◆◆◆◆◆◆◆◆◆◆◆◆◆

A common thread among the most fulfilled and happy individuals I know is their dedication to community service. Instead of asking, "What can the world give me?" they ask, "What can I offer the world?" This shift in perspective leads to a profound transformation, one that promotes a sustainable future while also enriching personal fulfillment.

Community-centric leadership goes beyond individual success. It is about recognizing that our collective well-being depends on our ability to work together, share resources, and support one another. This ethos fosters a sense of purpose and happiness by making a tangible difference in the lives of others. When we adopt this mindset, our actions contribute to shaping a better tomorrow, where everyone has a role in the community's success.

When leaders and entrepreneurs focus on what they can offer their communities, they set an example for others to follow. This creates a virtuous cycle, where the more we give, the more we receive in terms of trust, support, and cooperation. It fosters a culture of collaboration, where people are encouraged to contribute their skills and ideas for the common good.

Engaging with the local community is a critical strategy for businesses aiming to build strong relationships and promote organic growth. It involves more than just maintaining a presence in the area; it is about actively contributing to the community's well-being and establishing meaningful connections with local stakeholders. This approach demonstrates a genuine commitment to the people and places in your market.

Start by participating in local events such as fairs, charity fundraisers, and cultural festivals. These gatherings offer an opportunity to interact with community members personally, allowing you to understand their needs, interests, and values. By showing up and engaging with people in these settings, you create a positive image of your business and lay the foundation for long-term relationships.

Sponsoring community initiatives is another effective way to demonstrate your commitment. Consider supporting local schools, sports teams, or environmental projects. This not only provides tangible benefits to the community but also builds brand visibility and loyalty. When your business is seen as an active contributor to the local community, people are more likely to support your products and services.

I have been actively working to revitalize neighborhoods in my hometown through "Reimagine Memphis," an initiative to breathe new life into the community by transforming blighted areas into a vibrant, thriving place that residents proudly call home. Since returning to Memphis, I have been actively working on this initiative, particularly in my childhood neighborhood of Whitehaven. While the neighborhood is changing, it still has many good people who deserve quality housing, and I want to help them. By renovating homes, we are not only improving the physical landscape but also fostering a sense of pride and ownership among residents.

Attending town hall meetings and other local forums is also key to understanding the issues that matter most to your community. These meetings allow you to stay informed about local developments, voice your opinions, and collaborate with other stakeholders. By engaging in these discussions, you position your business as a responsible and informed community member.

I also contribute to my community by conducting first-time home-buying seminars. These seminars empower individuals and families with the knowledge and resources to navigate the buying process. By demystifying this often-daunting task, we are helping more people achieve the dream of homeownership, which in turn contributes to the stability and prosperity of our community.

Establishing strong partnerships with local businesses, suppliers, and subcontractors is another essential aspect of local engagement. These relationships not only boost the local economy but also create a network of reliable and supportive partners. When businesses work together, they can share resources, expertise, and contacts, leading to greater efficiency and innovation. This collaborative approach also opens doors to new opportunities and business ventures, fostering a spirit of mutual growth and success.

Beyond the practical benefits, local engagement fosters trust and goodwill. When people see your business actively involved in community activities and initiatives, it engenders a sense of loyalty and trust, which can lead to positive word-of-mouth reviews, increased customer retention, and a stronger reputation within the community.

Training Tomorrow's Workforce: A Community-Focused Approach

Initiating skill development programs, workshops, or apprenticeships for residents is a powerful way to foster community growth while also meeting the evolving demands of the construction industry. By collaborating with educational institutions to offer internships and training opportunities for students, you create a pipeline of skilled workers who are invested in the success of your projects and the broader community.

Skill development programs provide valuable training for individuals interested in construction-related careers. By offering workshops and apprenticeships, you give residents the tools and knowledge they need to succeed in various construction roles. These programs cover a range of skills, from carpentry and masonry to project management and safety practices. As participants acquire new skills, they become more employable, opening doors to stable and rewarding careers in construction.

Collaborations with schools, colleges, and vocational training centers can significantly expand the reach of your skill development initiatives. By working with educators, you can assist in designing courses that meet industry standards and provide students with hands-on experience. These partnerships not only benefit the students but also establish your business as a critical contributor to the community's educational and economic development.

Skill development programs and partnerships with educational institutions can also promote diversity and inclusion in the construction industry. By reaching out to under-represented groups and offering tailored training opportunities, you create a more diverse workforce. This inclusive approach brings a broader range of skills, ideas, and perspectives to your projects, enriching the industry and fostering a more equitable community.

Offering internships and apprenticeships allows students to gain real-world experience. These opportunities are invaluable for those looking to enter the industry, as they provide a chance to apply classroom knowledge in a practical setting. Interns and apprentices also bring fresh perspectives and enthusiasm to your projects, fostering innovation and a vibrant work culture.

Another initiative close to my heart is the She Builds Summer Camp for Girls, which I am currently developing and plan to launch in the near future. This program aims to inspire and empower young girls by introducing them to the construction world. Through hands-on activities and mentorship, we will teach valuable skills while challenging gender stereotypes and encouraging girls to explore careers in male-dominated fields. This initiative is about more than just skill-building; the goal is to instill confidence, promote equality, and shape the future leaders of our industry.

By investing in the development of local talent, you contribute to the economic growth and prosperity of the community. A skilled workforce attracts more businesses and creates a cycle of growth and development. It also reduces unemployment and empowers individuals to achieve their career and financial goals. When residents have the skills and opportunities to succeed, they are more likely to stay in the area, further strengthening the local economy.

Initiating skill development programs, workshops, or apprenticeships and collaborating with educational institutions is a win-win strategy. It empowers residents with valuable skills, supports community growth, and fosters a diverse and inclusive workforce. By investing in local talent, you contribute to the community's prosperity while building a solid foundation for the future success of your construction business.

Adopting Sustainable Construction Practices

The construction industry significantly impacts the environment, but by adopting sustainable practices, you can minimize this impact and contribute to a greener future. Engaging with the community to discuss and implement eco-friendly initiatives, such as energy-efficient building designs or waste reduction programs, fosters a sense of shared responsibility and can lead to innovative solutions.

Sustainable construction practices focus on reducing the industry's carbon footprint, conserving natural resources, and promoting energy efficiency. By using recycled materials, energy-efficient systems, and sustainable design principles, you can significantly reduce your projects' environmental impact. This not only benefits the planet but also aligns with growing consumer demand for eco-friendly products and services.

Engagement with the community is essential when implementing sustainable practices. By involving local stakeholders in discussions about eco-friendly initiatives, you create a sense of ownership and commitment to sustainability. Hosting community meetings, workshops, or open houses to discuss sustainability goals and gather feedback fosters a collaborative approach. This open dialogue can lead to creative ideas, local support, and increased awareness of the importance of sustainability in construction.

Energy-efficient building designs are a cornerstone of sustainable construction. By incorporating features such as solar panels, high-efficiency insulation, and energy-saving lighting and appliances, you can significantly reduce energy consumption and costs. These energy-efficient designs benefit the environment and contribute to long-term sustainability.

Construction projects often generate a considerable amount of waste. Developing waste reduction programs that prioritize recycling, reusing, and repurposing materials can help minimize the waste sent to landfills. Engaging the community in these programs by providing recycling stations, hosting clean-up events, and encouraging responsible waste management practices creates a collective effort toward sustainability.

By prioritizing sustainability in your construction practices, you showcase a commitment to the community's well-being and a greener future. This not only enhances your business's reputation but also attracts clients, partners, and employees who share similar values. Sustainability can become a key differentiator in a competitive industry, allowing your business to stand out and attract like-minded stakeholders.

Sustainable construction practices contribute to a greener future by reducing environmental impact and promoting responsible resource use. When businesses adopt these practices, they set a positive example for the rest of the industry and inspire others to follow suit. This collective effort can drive meaningful change and help address global environmental challenges.

The field of sustainable construction is continually evolving. It is important to be informed about new technologies, materials, and practices that can enhance sustainability. Attending industry conferences, participating in sustainability-focused workshops, and joining professional organizations dedicated to green building can provide valuable insights and help you maintain an innovative approach to sustainability.

Contributing to Community Welfare Through Philanthropy

Philanthropic activities are a meaningful way to contribute to community welfare and establish your business as a socially responsible organization. Supporting local charities, sponsoring educational programs, and participating in community clean-up efforts are just a few ways to engage with and uplift your community.

Supporting local charities is a direct way to give back to the community. Consider partnering with charitable organizations that align with your business values. This support can take many forms, such as financial donations, in-kind contributions, or volunteer efforts. By consistently supporting these charities, you help them expand their reach and make a more significant impact on those in need. This not only demonstrates your business's commitment to social responsibility but also fosters a sense of unity and shared purpose within the community.

Education is a cornerstone of community development. By sponsoring educational programs, you can play a pivotal role in nurturing the next generation. Consider supporting local schools, colleges, or community centers by providing scholarships, funding extracurricular activities, or donating educational materials. Sponsoring STEM programs, for instance, can inspire young people to pursue careers in construction and related fields. These initiatives create opportunities for learning and growth while establishing your business as a key contributor to the community's educational success.

Active participation in community clean-up efforts is a hands-on way to demonstrate your commitment to the environment and community welfare. Organize or join events such as park clean-ups, beach clean-ups, or neighborhood beautification projects. These activities not only improve the local environment but also bring people together for a common cause. By participating in these efforts, you show that your business is invested in maintaining a clean and healthy community, further solidifying your reputation as a responsible organization.

Contributing to community welfare through philanthropic activities helps build an impressive reputation for your business. When people see your commitment to supporting charities, sponsoring educational programs, and participating in clean-up efforts, they recognize that your organization genuinely cares about the community's well-being. This positive perception can lead to increased trust and new business opportunities.

Engaging in philanthropic activities can also foster a culture of giving within your organization. Encourage employees to volunteer, participate in charity events, and suggest new ways to give back to the community. This inclusive approach not only boosts employee morale but also strengthens the bond between your business and the community. When everyone in your organization shares a sense of purpose and commitment to social responsibility, it creates a more cohesive and motivated workforce.

Philanthropic activities contribute to long-term community welfare by addressing immediate needs and promoting positive change. By supporting charities, sponsoring education, and engaging in clean-up efforts, you help create a stronger, more resilient community. These contributions can have a lasting impact, leading to improved social cohesion, economic development, and environmental sustainability.

Embracing a community mindset is not only a strategic choice but also a commitment to sustainable growth and positive societal impact. Through local engagement, transparent communication, skill development programs, environmentally conscious practices, and social responsibility initiatives, entrepreneurs can forge lasting relationships that extend beyond project completion. By investing in the community, you create a foundation for long-term success and make a meaningful difference in people's lives.

TAKEAWAYS

◆ **Community-Centric Leadership:** This approach focuses on serving and connecting with communities. It fosters a sense of purpose and happiness by making a tangible difference in the lives of others.

◆ **Building Strong Local Connections:** Engaging with the local community is a critical business strategy. It involves participating in local events, sponsoring community initiatives, attending local forums, and establishing solid partnerships with local businesses.

◆ **Training Tomorrow's Workforce:** Initiating skill development programs, workshops, or apprenticeships for residents fosters community growth. Collaborating with educational institutions to offer internships and training opportunities creates a pipeline of skilled workers.

◆ **Adopting Sustainable Construction Practices:** Sustainable construction practices can minimize environmental impact and contribute to a greener future. It involves using recycled materials, energy-efficient systems, and sustainable design principles.

◆ **Contributing to Community Welfare through Philanthropy:** Philanthropic activities contribute to community welfare and establish businesses as socially responsible organizations. It involves supporting local charities, sponsoring educational programs, and participating in community clean-up efforts.

REFLECTIONS

☐ **Community-Centric Leadership:**
  ▶ How can you shift your perspective from "What can the world give me?" to "What can I offer the world?"
  ▶ What steps can you take to foster a culture of collaboration in your community or organization?

☐ **Building Strong Local Connections:**
  ▶ What local events or initiatives could you participate in to strengthen your connection with your community?
  ▶ How can you establish meaningful partnerships with local businesses, suppliers, and subcontractors?

☐ **Training Tomorrow's Workforce:**
  ▶ How can you contribute to skill development in your community?
  ▶ Are there local educational institutions you could collaborate with to offer internships or training opportunities?

☐ **Adopting Sustainable Practices:**
  ▶ What sustainable practices could you implement in your work or business?
  ▶ How can you engage your community in discussions about eco-friendly initiatives?

☐ **Contributing to Community Welfare through Philanthropy:**
  ▶ What philanthropic activities could you engage in to contribute to community welfare?
  ▶ How can you encourage a culture of giving within your organization?

Notes

PREFACE

[1] Rebecca Winke, *History of Women in Construction,* Family Handyman, December 8, 2023, https://www.familyhandyman.com/article/women-in-construction-history/.

[2] Parker Poe Adams & Bernstein LLP, *EEOC Releases Recommended Practices for Preventing Workplace Harassment in Construction Industry,* JDSupra, June 28, 2024, https://www.jdsupra.com/legalnews/eeoc-releases-recommended-practices-for-6056350/.

[3] *Women in Engineering,* Engineering UK, accessed May 23, 2024, https://www.engineeringuk.com/media/318036/women-in-engineering-report-extended-analysis-engineeringuk-march-2022.pdf.

[4] *Only Around 1 in 5 Space Industry Workers are Women,* UN News, October 4, 2021, https://news.un.org/en/story/2021/10/1102082.

[5] Michele Lytle, Robin Wagner Skarbek, and Ryan Robinson, *Shifting Diversity into High Gear,* Deloitte Insights, May 30, 2019, https://www2.deloitte.com/us/en/insights/industry/automotive/women-in-automotive-sector-gender-diversity.html.

CHAPTER 5 | The Transformative Power of a Growth Mindset

[1] Dweck, Carol S. *Mindset: The New Psychology of Success.* Ballatine Books, 2007.

[2] Piper, W. (2001). *The Little Engine That Could.* G P Putnam's Sons.

CHAPTER 6 | A Multifaceted Approach to Empower Women

[1] Grant, Adam. *Think Again.* Penguin Audio, 2021.

[2] Ivan Misner, David Alexander, Brian Hilliard. *Networking Like a Pro: Turning Contacts into Connections.* Entrepreneur Press, 2017.

CHAPTER 7 | Constructing a Network: The Influence of Inspirational Figures, Mentors, Allies and Sponsors

[1] Hewlett, Sylvia Ann. *Forget a Mentor, Find a Sponsor.* Brighton: Harvard Business Review Press, 2013.

[2] Catlin, Karen. *Better Allies: Everyday Actions to Create Inclusive, Engaging Workplaces.* San Mateo: Karen Catlin Consulting, 2019.

CHAPTER 8 | Navigating Imposter Syndrome, Sexism, and Microaggressions

[1] Paulise, Luciana. *75% of Women Executives Experience Imposter Syndrome in the Workplace.* 8 March 2023. <https://www.forbes.com/sites/lucianapaulise/2023/03/08/75-of-women-executives-experience-imposter-syndrome-in-the-workplace/?sh=4de967916899>.

[2] Heaton, Kimbely Riddle and Karen. *Antecedents to Sexual Harassment of Women in Selected Male-Dominated Occupations: A Systematic Review.* 4 April 2023. <https://pubmed.ncbi.nlm.nih.gov/37016801/>.

[3] Washington, Ella F. *Recognizing and Responding to Microaggressions at Work.* 10 May 2022.<https://hbr.org/2022/05/recognizing-and-responding-to-microaggressions-at-work>.

CHAPTER 9 | Unlocking Success Through Emotional Intelligence

[1] Greaves, Travis Bradberry and Jean. *Emotional Intelligence 2.0.* Talent Smart, 2009.

[2] *Economic Impact Report.* 2021. <https://wttc.org/research/economic-impact>.

[3] Bagalini, Adwoa. *5 Ways Intersectionality Affects Diversity and Inclusion at Work.* 22 July 2020. <https://www.weforum.org/agenda/2020/07/diversity-inclusion-equality-intersectionality/>.

[4] Bradberry, Travis. *Emotional Intelligence Habits: How to Manage Your Emotions, Improve Your Relationships, and Increase Your EQ*. Talent Smart, 2023.

CHAPTER 11 | From Glass Ceilings to Growth – Celebrating Female Leadership

[1] Hernandez, Nick. *"Because I Said So": Why Top-Down Management Doesn't Work*. 30 March 2024. <https://360learning.com/blog/top-down-management/#id-2-top-down-management-stifles-talent-and-curiosity>.

[2] Guerrier, M. (n.d.). *About - HerSuiteSpot*. Retrieved from HerSuiteSpot website.

[3] Hewlett, S. A., Marshall, M., & Sherbin, L. (2013). *How Diversity Can Drive Innovation*. Harvard Business Review, 91(12), 30–31.

[4] Hewlett, S.A., Marshall, M. (2013). *Forget a Mentor, Find a Sponsor: The New Way to Fast-Track Your Career*. Brighton: Harvard Buisness Review Press.

[5] Jansen, Corine. *Sex Differences in Listening*. April 2024.

[6] Rivera, Jessica. *Mastering Strategic Communication*. 30 March 2024. <www.jrcoaching.net>.

[7] Court, Dominic Barton adn David. *Three Keys to Building a Data-Driven Strategy*. 1 March 2013. <https://www.mckinsey.com/capabilities/mckinsey-digital/our-insights/three-keys-to-building-a-data-driven-strategy>.

CHAPTER 12 | Mastering Communication Skills

[1] Younger, H. R. (2023). *The Art of Active Listening: How People at Work Feel Heard, Valued, and Understood*. Berrett-Koehler Publishers.

[2] Stone, D., Patton, B., & Heen, S. (1999). *Difficult Conversations: How to Discuss What Matters Most*. Penguin Books.

[3] Danesi, M. (2021). *Understanding Nonverbal Communication: A Semiotic Guide*. Bloomsbury Academic.

APPENDIX

Blueprint Example

◆◆◆◆◆◆◆◆◆◆◆◆◆◆

Following is an example of a blueprint for professional success in the construction industry. It emphasizes how dedication, persistence, and strategic planning (short and long-term goals) can be used to make meaningful contributions to the industry.

1. **Self-Assessment and Skill Development:**

   Conduct a comprehensive self-assessment to identify strengths, skills, and areas for improvement relevant to the construction industry.

   Seek opportunities for skill development, such as enrolling in construction management courses, gaining hands-on experience through internships or apprenticeships, and obtaining relevant certifications.

2. **Education and Training:**

   Pursue a degree in construction management or a related field to build a strong foundation of knowledge and expertise.

   Actively participate in workshops, seminars, and industry conferences to stay updated on the latest trends, technologies, and best practices in construction.

3. **Networking and Relationship Building:**

   Cultivate a robust professional network by attending industry events, joining construction associations, and connecting with peers, mentors, and industry leaders.

   Seek opportunities to collaborate on projects, volunteer for industry initiatives, and participate in mentorship programs to expand the network and gain valuable insights.

4. **Professional Experience and Leadership Development:**

   Seek opportunities to gain hands-on experience in various aspects of the construction process, from project management to site supervision.

   Actively seek leadership roles within organizations, taking on responsibilities that demonstrate the ability to lead teams, solve problems, and deliver results.

5. **Brand Building and Thought Leadership:**

   Share knowledge, expertise, and insights through various channels, such as blogs, articles, podcasts, and public speaking engagements, to establish yourself as a thought leader in the construction industry.

   Leverage social media platforms and professional networks to showcase projects, achievements, and contributions to the industry to position yourself as a trusted authority and influencer.

6. **Business Development and Entrepreneurship:**

   Explore opportunities to start a construction firm or consultancy, leveraging expertise, network, and reputation to attract clients and grow the business.

   Develop a strategic business plan, identifying target markets, competitive advantages, and growth opportunities to guide entrepreneurial endeavors.

7. **Advocacy and Community Engagement:**

   Advocate for diversity, equity, and inclusion in the construction industry, championing initiatives to increase representation and support for women and underrepresented groups.

   Actively engage with community organizations, educational institutions, and government agencies to promote workforce development, apprenticeship programs, and opportunities for aspiring professionals in construction.

Acknowledgments

◆◆◆◆◆◆◆◆◆◆◆◆◆

I am grateful as I reflect on the incredible journey chronicled within these pages. I am humbled by the unwavering support and inspiration from those nearest and dearest to me.

To our son, **Darby Ross**, you were my first spark of motivation and continue to be one of the driving forces behind my pursuit of a life without limits. Your resilience and zest for life remind me daily of the boundless possibilities that await.

To **Devon Ross**, our son with a heart as vast as the calmest river, thank you for your kindness and serenity. In moments of chaos, your presence brings peace.

To my bonus children, **Kay and Nina Ross**, you have enriched my life in countless ways. You are not merely a part of my life but an integral part of who I am.

And lastly, to our wonderful daughters-in-law, **Toddreanna and Kristen Ross**, your love and support have been invaluable. Your presence completes our family circle, and I am grateful for the bonds we share.

To my parents, **Elgin and Gloria Teal**, your unwavering commitment to integrity and hard work has been my guiding light. Your example helped to shape my character. I am profoundly grateful for the values you instilled in me and the foundation you provided for my journey.

To my brother, **Reginald Thompson**, and my sister, **Anitra Fulton**, you have been my steadfast cheerleaders throughout every twist and turn. I am grateful for the warmth of your support and the strength of our familial bond.

To my brother-in-law, **Nikita Ross**, and sister-in-law, **Jowanna Ross**, your roles in my life extend far beyond the bounds of traditional in-law relationships. You have welcomed me into your lives as a sister, offering unwavering support and encouragement throughout the years.

To my dearest friends, **Ethan and Tamala Gladney, Monique Hunt, Mary Simpson, Lisa Howell**, and countless others whose names fill my heart with gratitude—your unwavering friendship has illuminated my life's journey, infusing it with richness and meaning.

I extend my heartfelt gratitude to our dedicated publisher, **Patricia Potts**, and the **National Association of Home Builders**. Your steadfast commitment to fostering diversity and belief in the power of my dedication to its publication have made this journey all the more fulfilling.

To each person mentioned here and to the countless others who have touched my life, thank you for being part of this remarkable journey. Your impact is immeasurable, and this acknowledgment is a small tribute to the profound gratitude that resides in my heart.

About the Author

Tammie Ross is the Chief Executive Officer and General Contractor of Residence by Ross. She is the architect of a vision that transforms houses into homes and dreams into blueprints. Her leadership is the cornerstone of a minority woman-owned burgeoning empire in the construction industry that is proudly and resolutely committed to excellence.

Her educational journey is evidence of her dedication to mastery and precision. She is a cum laude graduate of Christian Brothers University and a graduate of Louisiana State University, where she earned her MBA in Project Management with distinction. Her certification further highlights her pursuit of continuous improvement as a Six Sigma Green Belt Professional, a reflection of her strategic acumen and her proficiency in enhancing business processes.

Before laying the foundations of her company, Tammie charted a remarkable 20-year career in the financial sector, specializing in automotive financing. Her roles have been diverse and impactful, ranging from Regional Sales Director to Vice President of Business Controls and Risk Management to Director of Strategic Partners. Her real estate tenure is equally impressive, spanning over 18 years and decorated with accolades, underscoring her expertise in property markets and client advocacy.

Tammie's mission is to inspire and encourage women and girls to ascend to new heights in traditionally male-dominated fields. Her presence in the construction sector catalyzes change, fostering an environment where diversity is welcomed and celebrated.